THE GREEN–FINGERED GARDENER
seasonal kitchen gardening

THE GREEN-FINGERED GARDENER

seasonal kitchen gardening

a practical guide to gardening for produce throughout the year

peter mchoy

southwater

This edition is published by Southwater

Southwater is an imprint of Anness Publishing Ltd
Hermes House, 88–89 Blackfriars Road, London SE1 8HA
tel. 020 7401 2077; fax 020 7633 9499
www.southwaterbooks.com; info@anness.com

© Anness Publishing Ltd 2000, 2003

UK agent: The Manning Partnership Ltd
6 The Old Dairy, Melcombe Road, Bath BA2 3LR
tel. 01225 478444; fax 01225 478440; sales@manning-partnership.co.uk

UK distributor: Grantham Book Services Ltd
Isaac Newton Way, Alma Park Industrial Estate, Grantham, Lincs NG31 9SD
tel. 01476 541080; fax 01476 541061; orders@gbs.tbs-ltd.co.uk

North American agent/distributor: National Book Network
4501 Forbes Boulevard, Suite 200, Lanham, MD 20706
tel. 301 459 3366; fax 301 429 5746; www.nbnbooks.com

Australian agent/distributor: Pan Macmillan Australia
Level 18, St Martins Tower, 31 Market St, Sydney, NSW 2000
tel. 1300 135 113; fax 1300 135 103; customer.service@macmillan.com.au

New Zealand agent/distributor: David Bateman Ltd
30 Tarndale Grove, Off Bush Road, Albany, Auckland
tel. (09) 415 7664; fax (09) 415 8892

A CIP catalogue record for this book is available from the British Library.

Publisher: Joanna Lorenz
Project Editors: Jeremy Smith & Emma Hardy
Production Controller: Darren Price
Designers: Mark Latter, Patrick Mcleavey & Jo Brewer
Photographer: Peter Anderson
Illustrator: Michael Shoebridge

Previously published as *The Seasonal Kitchen Garden*

1 3 5 7 9 10 8 6 4 2

■ PAGE ONE
Leeks and curly kale
compete for space in this
vegetable garden, planted
with an array of crops.

■ PAGE TWO
The union of vegetables
and flowers in this
exuberant potager results
in a profusion of colour.

■ PAGE THREE
In this vegetable plot,
crops are grown in orderly
rows, which is a popular
method of growing
vegetables.

■ ABOVE
A greenhouse can be
decorative in its own
right as well as providing
warmth and shelter
to crops.

■ RIGHT
Beautiful, wonderfully
wholesome fare that can
go straight from the
vegetable plot to the
dinner table.

CONTENTS

INTRODUCTION

ABOVE: *Turnips are a hardy vegetable that can be grown all year round.*

In the past, when self-sufficiency was a way of life, people seemed to instinctively know how to grow good, nutritious produce on their own land. The relationship between man and soil was symbiotic, a partnership, and gardeners had a real feel for the land they worked on. In today's frenetic age, we have lost that special relationship to a degree, but self-sufficiently is becoming increasingly in vogue. As we become more aware of the chemicals that modern farming practices use to treat our produce, the demand for organic produce steadily increases. The promise of naturally wholesome foods has become increasingly alluring, and more and more of us are undertaking to grow our own food for the dinner table.

ABOVE: *Wonderfully tempting fruit such as raspberries can be grown in gardens of all sizes.*

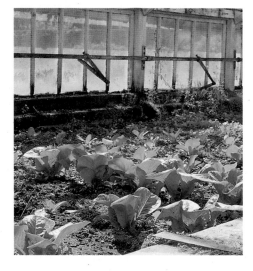

ABOVE: *A greenhouse makes a delightful feature and could double your productivity.*

This book provides practical, down-to-earth help and advice that will help you to make your garden start producing for you. To combat the vagaries of the weather, jobs are arranged by seasons, rather than conforming to a rigid timetable. Extended summers can quickly turn into premature winters that may wreak havoc on your crops, so keep an eye on the weather rather than letting yourself be ruled by the calendar. The checklists for each season can be used as a guide, but allow some slack in case of climatic irregularities. Information is provided on when to plant crops and when the various vegetables

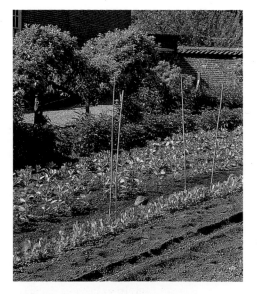

ABOVE: *Young vegetables will thrive in carefully prepared soil that is kept in good condition.*

are best harvested. Advice is also given on how to grow early crops with the aid of cloches, cold frames and greenhouses.

The book begins with spring, the real start of a gardener's year. This section is filled with the activities of planting and sowing, laying the groundwork to ensure a fruitful harvest-time. Step by step, you will discover how to apply organic material such as manure, how to warm the soil with cloches, and how to sow the maincrop vegetables. There is also useful advice on handy techniques practised by experienced gardeners, such as fluid sowing and checking the quality of your soil.

In summer, the book tells you which crops should be sown, how to thin out vegetables sown in spring, how to summer prune fruits, and offers advice about spotting and stopping garden pests.

During autumn, take advantage of mild spells to get out in the garden and carry out the few really pressing jobs of the year. Lift onions and potatoes to store, protect low-growing vegetables with cloches and service the greenhouse before the chill of winter sets in.

Winter is a time for planning ahead, and the book suggests tasks that would be beneficial in preparing the garden for new growth the following spring. Testing soil, winter-digging the vegetable plot and other tasks will all ensure that your garden is ready to cope with even the most arduous of winters, while you can also begin to sow early crops such as radishes and turnips.

LEFT: *Divided plants can grow for a good three seasons before propagation needs to be repeated.*

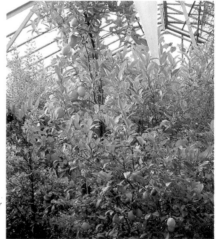

RIGHT: *A colourful greenhouse protects from inclement weather a variety of fruit and vegetable plants.*

LEFT: *A harvest boon like this crop of beautiful apples makes all that hard work seem worthwhile.*

RIGHT: *To retain their aromatic qualities, herbs should be dried as slowly as possible.*

PLANNING YOUR KITCHEN GARDEN

These days kitchen gardens are not only expected to be productive, they are also expected to look good. Besides being pleasing to the eye, a well-designed kitchen garden has many practical advantages. It will help you to plan your vegetable growing so that your garden will remain productive throughout the year, and it will help you to decide what varieties to grow and how much seed you will need.

Keep the design as simple as possible, and make sure that you select a site that receives a lot of sunlight and drains well. Kitchen gardens are

ABOVE: *Apples are one of the most widely grown fruit.*

TOP: *Fruit trees add elegance to any garden.*

LEFT: *In small gardens, vegetables such as broad beans are ideal because they can be trained upwards so that they take up less space.*

OPPOSITE: *Sage makes a highly attractive plant for the border as well as a useful herb for the kitchen garden.*

achievable in gardens of all sizes. Vegetables that are hungry for space, such as potatoes and cabbages, are more suited to the larger garden. But if you are content with smaller vegetables such as lettuces, carrots and dwarf beans, and can relegate climbing beans and expansive plants like artichokes to the mixed or herbaceous border, it is quite practical to grow a wide range of vegetables even where space is quite restricted.

If you have a reasonably sized garden – large enough to divide off a section for a kitchen garden – growing in the ground rather than pots or growing bags is the best way to produce your vegetables and fruit.

Fruit trees and bushes are often ornamental and can be easily integrated into the flower garden. Trained fruit trees, such as espalier and fan apples, are attractive even in winter.

Herbs are much more easily accommodated than vegetables. Many are highly ornamental and lots of them make good container plants. Others look perfectly in place in a border. If you want to make a real feature of your herbs, make a herb garden a key part of your design.

FRUIT IN A SMALL SPACE

The most satisfactory way to grow tree fruits such as apples and pears in a small garden or a confined space is trained as a cordon, fan or espalier against a wall or fence. Even some bush fruits such as gooseberries can be trained as cordons or double cordons against a fence.

ABOVE: *Wall-trained fruit trees take up relatively little space.*
RIGHT: *If you want apples in a small garden it is best to use one of the columnar varieties or to grow an ordinary variety on a trained system like this espalier 'Lord Lambourne'.*

Blackberries and hybrid berries can be trained against a fence or over an arch, but keep the growth contained and avoid allowing thorny shoots to overhang pathways.

It is even possible to grow apples in pots on the patio, but with the new flagpole-type varieties available that grow in a narrow column, you may prefer to plant these where space is limited. They will require much less watering and attention than ordinary varieties on dwarfing rootstocks in pots.

The initial training of espaliers, fans and cordons demands patience and skill. Unless you particularly like the challenge and can wait for two or three years longer, it is best to buy a ready-trained tree.

BUYING FRUIT TREES

Whether a fruit tree such as an apple, peach or cherry is suitable for a small garden depends not so much on the variety of the fruit but on the rootstock. This has a profound affect on the size of the tree (as well as how soon it starts to fruit). Always check the root-stock before you buy, and if in doubt ask whether it is suitably dwarfing for a small garden.

TRAINED FRUIT TREES

Trained trees look attractive and produce a heavy crop from a restricted space. But they require regular and methodical training, sometimes twice a year. If in doubt about how to prune a particular trained fruit, consult an encyclopedia or fruit book.

Espaliers are more ornamental than cordons (some shrubs, such as pyracanthas, are occasionally trained as espaliers using the same methods).

Cordons are usually trained at an angle of about 45 degrees, secured to support canes and wires fixed to stout posts or to a fence. Many plants can be planted in a small space, and soft fruits such as gooseberries and red and white currants can be trained in this way, saving the space taken up by a bush form.

Fans can be free-standing, tied to wires supported by posts, but they are usually planted against a wall or fence. In time a fan can be trained to cover a large area, such as a garage wall.

Step-overs are single-tiered espaliers, used as a fruiting edging, perhaps within the kitchen garden.

Potted fruit

Apples can be grown in pots provided you choose a very dwarfing rootstock. The same applies to peaches. You can experiment with other bush and tree fruits, but bear in mind that this is second best to growing them in the ground.

Flagpole apples

You can buy a range of apple trees that rarely produce long sideshoots, but instead grow upright and produce most fruiting spurs along the main vertical stem. These take up little space and won't cast a heavy shadow, so they are ideal for growing in a flower bed. The blossom is pretty in spring, and the ripening fruits are ornamental later in the year.

Rhubarb

Rhubarb is ornamental enough to be grown in the flower border. You can even grow it in a large pot as a foliage plant for the patio, though this is not the best way to achieve a heavy crop.

ABOVE: *This rhubarb chard is growing in a flower bed.*

Strawberries

If you don't have much space for fruit, at least try growing strawberries. A strawberry barrel or a tower container will hold a lot of strawberries and provided you keep the container well watered it will be laden with fruit . . . which won't

ABOVE: *There is always space for a few strawberries if you grow them in a container like this.*

become splashed with mud if the weather is wet or awkward to pick. Also the fruit will be more difficult for slugs to reach.

FINDING ROOM FOR VEGETABLES

If you are really restricted for space, and the lure of fresh home-grown vegetables is strong, you can grow them in containers. Wherever possible, however, it is better to grow them in the ground.

If you simply don't have space for a vegetable plot, quite a lot of vegetables can be grown in beds and borders intermixed with ornamental plants.

The 'vegetable plot' should never be tucked away in a dull, sunless part of the garden. Most vegetables need good light and plenty of moisture to do well. Dry ground shaded by hedges and walls seldom produces succulent vegetables.

Among the flowers

It is quite possible to incorporate vegetables as part of a formal bedding scheme – red or purple rhubarb chard leaves contrast well with grey foliaged bedding plants, carrot foliage doesn't look unattractive as a foil for bright summer bedding plants, and even a red or green leaved cut-and-come-again (oak leaf) lettuce such as 'Salad Bowl' will make a pretty edging for a bed of summer bedding. Unfortunately the problem comes at harvest time. When gaps soon become rather conspicuous in a formal bedding scheme.

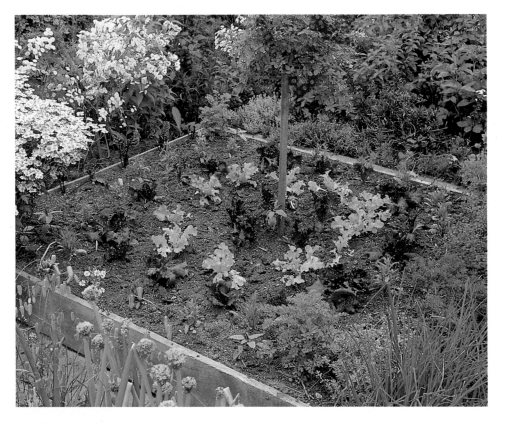

ABOVE: *This raised vegetable bed in a flower garden makes an interesting feature as well as a productive area.*

LEFT: *Ornamental kales are usually grown for their decorative effect, but they are edible if you get tired of looking at them! This variety is 'Coral Queen'.*

Vegetables are more acceptable as gap fillers in the herbaceous or mixed border. They fill the space admirably, and after harvesting the border is left no less attractive than it was originally. Suitable candidates are lettuces, radishes, beetroot, asparagus, peas, carrots, leaf beet and spinach but much depends on the size of the space and your imagination.

Ornamental potagers

The term potager comes from *jardin potager*, simply being French for kitchen garden. But the term has come to refer primarily to a kitchen garden – usually with both fruit and vegetables – laid out ornamentally, perhaps with beds edged with low hedges like a parterre. Treated like this, your kitchen garden can become a prominent design element in the small garden.

Growing bags

Growing bags are excellent for vegetables if all you have is a balcony or patio on which to grow them. It is quite feasible to grow lettuces, spinach, radishes, cucumbers, tomatoes, turnips, even self-blanching celery and potatoes, in growing bags.

Clearly, you won't keep the family fed with potatoes from a couple of growing bags, and the economics don't make much sense. But it is worth planting an early variety (you can always move the bag into a protected area if frost threatens) so that you can enjoy those first few new potatoes straight from the garden . . . or patio . . . or balcony.

ABOVE: *These are 'Totem' tomatoes growing in a 25cm (10in) pot.*

BELOW: *You can even grow tomatoes in a hanging basket.*

Dwarf peas, another unlikely-sounding crop, can also be grown successfully in a growing bag.

Troughs, tubs and pots

Tomatoes are one of the most successful crops for a growing bag, and they are equally successful in pots provided you choose a suitable compact variety.

Courgettes and cucumbers are also a practical choice for a tub or large pot. Potatoes can be grown in a large pot for a bit of fun, but you might be better planting an aubergine or pepper in it.

Windowboxes and baskets

The only vegetable likely to do well in a hanging basket is the tomato, but you must choose a trailing or drooping variety, and maintain excellent control over both watering and feeding.

Windowboxes offer more scope, and apart from tomatoes (again, a dwarf or trailing variety is essential), stump-rooted carrots, radishes, onions, and lettuces are among the crops that do well.

Rather than grow a hearting lettuce, which leaves a gap as the whole head is harvested at once, try a non-hearting, cut-and-come-again variety that you can harvest in stages.

SPRING

As the chill of winter begins to ebb slowly away, gardeners need no persuasion to get out into the garden. Spring is a time of genesis for the garden, a time for sowing and laying the groundwork for a harvest boon all year round. You can also start to think about design in your kitchen garden. Opting to grow vegetables needn't mean condemning your garden to a life of dowdiness. Rows of vegetables such as purple broccoli can look extremely striking, and less demonstrative crops can be interspersed with more showy plants to create an attractive, less formal garden design.

Keep a watchful eye on the weather before starting work. A seemingly clement spring might soon lapse into a prolonged winter that could wreck your plans for the year ahead.

ABOVE: *Sowing vegetables in rows is a design formula that has stood the test of time.*

OPPOSITE: *A model kitchen garden plot, filled with leeks, cabbages, broccoli and other vegetables.*

EARLY SPRING

IN COLD REGIONS THE WEATHER can still be icy in early spring, but in many mild climates you can make a start on a range of outdoor jobs. If sowing or planting outdoors, keep an eye on soil temperature. Few seeds will germinate if the soil temperature is below 7°C (45°F), so use a soil thermometer to check before you sow.

JOBS IN BRIEF

The Kitchen Garden

❏ Apply manures and fertilizers to vegetable beds

❏ Plant onion sets and shallots

❏ Sow early crops such as summer radishes in cold frames or beneath cloches

❏ Start sowing vegetables without protection if you live in a mild area. Many kinds can be sown from early spring onwards, so check the packets as some varieties are more suitable than others for sowing

❏ Plant blackcurrant, red and white currant and gooseberry bushes.

❏ Chit or sprout potatoes ready to plant in mid-spring

❏ Use horticultural fleece or floating cloches to protect early crops if you don't have conventional cloches

❏ Apply fertilizer to fruit bushes if they need it

❏ Plant new strawberries, but make sure that they are healthy and disease-free

❏ Put cloches over strawberries if you want an early crop

The Greenhouse and Conservatory

❏ Sow greenhouse tomatoes in modules or pots until mid spring

❏ Sow aubergines (eggplant) in modules or pots indoors. Soak the seed in water overnight first. Aubergines can also be planted in containers and moved outside when the weather is warm

❏ Sow peppers in a propagator, set at about 18°c (65°f). They can be sown in individual pots or trays

❏ Increase ventilation on warm days

❏ Check plants for signs of pests and diseases, which multiply as the temperatures rise

TOP: *A dibber can be used to help plant out crops such as shallots.*

RIGHT: *Early spring is the ideal time to add manure and fertilizers where appropriate.*

CROPS IN SEASON

- ❑ **Broccoli** (for details on harvesting, see late winter).
- ❑ **Carrots** (for details on harvesting, see mid summer).
- ❑ **Celeriac** (for details on harvesting, see mid autumn).
- ❑ **Chard** (for details on harvesting, see late summer).
- ❑ **Chicory** (for details on harvesting, see mid to early winter).
- ❑ **Kale** (for details on harvesting, see late autumn).
- ❑ **Leeks** (for details on harvesting, see mid autumn).
- ❑ **Lettuces** (for details on harvesting, see late spring and early winter).

TOP RIGHT: *Leeks.*
BOTTOM LEFT: *Purple sprouting broccoli.*
BOTTOM RIGHT: *Kale planted in a row.*

PLANT ONION SETS

The biggest onions are usually grown from seed, but unless you can give them the dedicated care they need the results will be disappointing. Sets (small onion bulbs) are an almost foolproof way to grow onions, and you should be rewarded with a reasonable crop for very little effort.

1 Take out a shallow drill with the corner of a hoe or rake, using a garden line for a straight row. Space the sets about 15cm (6in) apart.

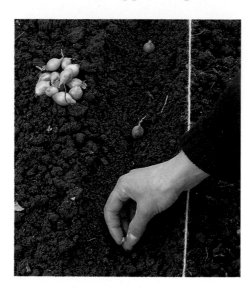

2 Pull the soil back over the drill, but leave the tips of the onions protruding. If birds are a problem – they may try to pull the onions out by the wispy old stems – protect with netting or keep pushing the bulbs back until rooted.

PLANT SHALLOTS

Shallots are useful for pickling, but also store well for use like onions. They are almost always grown from bulbs, bought or saved from last year's crop.

1 Planted in the same way as onion sets, shallots are spaced about 15cm (6in) apart, but the bulbs are larger, so the drill might have to be a little deeper. Push the bulbs into the base of the drill so that the tip is just protruding. Pull the soil back round them with a hoe or rake.

2 Shallots are useful for an early crop, and you can usually plant them outdoors in late winter, except in very cold regions. If you missed the winter planting but still want to get them growing quickly, start them off in individual pots.

3 Keep the pots in a cold frame or greenhouse until the shoots are 3–5cm (1–2in) high. Then plant the sprouted shallots in the garden, spacing them about 15cm (6in) apart.

SOW EARLY VEGETABLES OUTDOORS

Early sowing can be a gamble. If the weather is cold the seeds may rot before they germinate, and some vegetables tend to run to seed if they are subject to very cold conditions after germinating.

Concentrate early sowings on hardy crops like broad beans and early peas. Try a few short rows of a wider range of vegetables, but be prepared to resow if they don't do well.

 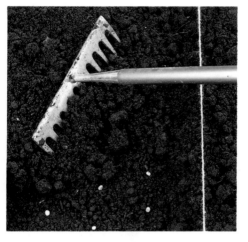

1 Peas are best sown in multiple rows so that they can support each other, with walking space between the double or triple rows. Broad beans are also often grown in multiple rows. Take out a flat-bottomed drill 5–8cm (2–3in) deep.

2 Space the seeds by hand. Peas are often sown in three staggered rows, spacing the seeds about 4cm (1½in) apart, but you can double this space and still get a good crop. Broad beans are sown in two rows with each seed about 23cm (9in) apart.

3 Pull the soil back over the drill to cover the seeds. If the ground is dry, water well until the seedlings are through. If seed-eaters such as mice are a problem, netting or traps may be necessary.

AN EARLY START

Peas and beans germinate readily in warm soil, but are less reliable in early spring when the soil temperature fluctuates. You can be more sure of your early peas if you start the seeds off in a greenhouse or cold frame first, then plant them out when they are growing well.

1 A length of old gutter is ideal for starting off the seeds. Block the ends and fill with soil.

2 Sow the seeds about 5–8cm (2–3in) apart, cover, then keep warm and moist.

3 When ready to plant out, take out a shallow drill with a draw hoe, and gradually slide the peas out of the gutter and into the row.

FERTILIZE THE VEGETABLE PLOT

The vegetable plot needs regular feeding if yields are not to suffer. Unlike beds and borders in the ornamental garden, little natural recycling occurs. The crops are removed and leaves do not naturally fall and decay. Bulky organic manures do much to improve soil structure and increase the nutrient-holding capabilities of the soil, but unless you follow an intensive organic approach and apply sufficient manures and garden compost, some chemical fertilizers are necessary if you want a heavy crop.

INDIVIDUAL BOOSTERS

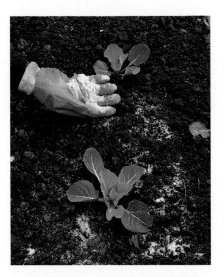

Throughout the growing season, certain vegetables may need boosters from specific fertilizers or quick-acting general fertilizers whenever growth seems to need encouraging. Spring cabbages often benefit from a light dressing of a nitrogenous fertilizer to stimulate the growth of fresh young leaves now that the weather is improving. Fruit crops, such as tomatoes, benefit from a high-potash feed.

1 The quickest way to apply a general fertilizer to your vegetable plot is with a wheeled spreader that you can adjust to deliver the appropriate amount. Calculate and test the delivery rate first.

2 If applying by hand, measure out the amount of fertilizer required for a square metre or yard, so that you can visualize how much you need. Or pour it into a small container as a measure and note how full it is.

3 Mark out metre or yard widths with strings, then use a couple of canes to divide these into metre or yard squares. When one square has been applied, move the back cane forward to mark out the next area.

4 Use your measure to scoop up the appropriate amount of fertilizer (use the application rates advised on the packet as a guide), then scatter it evenly. Hold the hand about 15–23cm (6–9in) above the soil.

5 Always rake the fertilizer into the surface. This spreads it more evenly and helps it to penetrate more rapidly.

HORTICULTURAL FLEECE

Horticultural fleece is a material that a previous generation of gardeners didn't possess, but the fact that it is now widely used commercially is evidence of its usefulness. The fleece will warm up the soil rather like a cloche, and should provide protection from a degree or two of frost. It also offers protection from animals such as rabbits and pests such as butterflies. You can use it just to start off your seeds, or as protection for a growing crop.

1 Sow your seeds then cover the area with the fleece. Anchor it down loosely with bricks or stones initially, while you secure the edges.

FLOATING CLOCHES

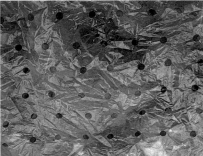

Other types of protective covers can also be used successfully. Some are very fine, long-lasting nets (see top), which give little frost protection but effectively keep out most animals and pests; others are perforated plastic films (see above) that let rain through and 'give' enough to rise with the growing crop.

You will have to pull them back to weed and thin. You will find that weeds thrive with the protection as well as the crops!

2 You can secure the edges with soil. Make a slit to tuck the end into, or just heap soil over the edges. Water will flow through the fleece, and it will also stretch a little as the plants grow.

3 You can buy various designs of proprietary pegs to hold the fleece in position, and these are preferable to the soil method as they make it easier to lift and replace the fleece for weeding and other cultivation tasks.

MID SPRING

FOR MANY GARDENERS MID SPRING is the most exciting as well as the busiest time of the year. Seedlings and cuttings are growing fast, and outdoor sowing and planting can begin in earnest. This is often a time to prioritize jobs. If you don't know whether something can wait, check for the late spring Jobs in Brief notes.

JOBS IN BRIEF

The Kitchen Garden

- ❑ Apply manures and fertilizers
- ❑ Plant onion sets
- ❑ Plant asparagus crowns
- ❑ Continue to sow in cold frames or beneath cloches for earlier crops
- ❑ Start sowing vegetables without protection. Many kinds can be sown from mid spring onwards, so check the packets
- ❑ If you don't have conventional cloches, use horticultural fleece or floating cloches for early crops
- ❑ Plant out vegetable seedlings such as cabbages
- ❑ Apply fertilizer to fruit bushes if they need it
- ❑ Plant new strawberries
- ❑ Put cloches over strawberries if you want an early crop
- ❑ Potatoes can be planted out now in most areas

The Greenhouse and Conservatory

- ❑ Sow tender vegetables such as outdoor tomatoes and runner beans to plant out later, and cucumbers for the greenhouse

TOP LEFT: *Cloches can be used to bring strawberries on earlier.*

TOP RIGHT: *Before planting, potatoes are usually "chitted" or sprouted.*

RIGHT: *In mid spring vulnerable crops may still need to be protected with horticultural fleece.*

CROPS IN SEASON

- **Asparagus** Cut just beneath the surface of the soil when the spears are 12–18cm (5–7in) high. Asparagus deteriorates quickly so eat as soon as possible.
- **Broccoli** (for details on harvesting, see late winter).
- **Cabbages** The leaves of spring cabbages are cut as required, a few being left to heart up if necessary (for details on harvesting, see late autumn).
- **Celeriac** (for details on harvesting, see mid autumn).
- **Chard** (for details on harvesting, see late summer).
- **Lettuces** (for details on harvesting, see late spring and early winter).
- **Rhubarb** Pull the stems rather than cutting them, always leaving at least four. Do not pull any stems after mid summer to give the plant a chance to replenish itself.
- **Summer radishes** are ready from mid spring onwards. They should be eaten as soon as possible.

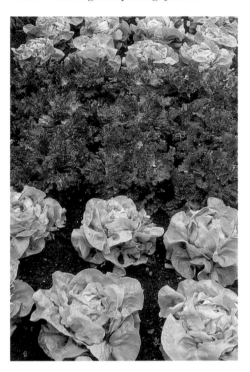

BELOW: *Block vegetable planting of lettuce.*

BELOW: *Harvesting asparagus.*

BELOW: *Harvesting rhubarb.*

BELOW: *Cabbages growing in a row.*

SOW MAINCROP VEGETABLES OUTDOORS

Vegetable sowing begins in earnest now, with crops like beetroot, spinach beet, summer cabbages, salad and pickling onions, scorzonera and turnips, as well as further sowings of lettuces, peas, radishes, spinach, carrots and cauliflowers. Dwarf beans can be sown in mild areas.

1 Break the soil down into a fine crumbly structure, and level with a rake before sowing.

2 Heavy soils may be difficult to break down into a fine structure with the rake, especially if the soil is dry. Treading on the largest lumps usually helps to break them down.

3 Once the soil is reasonably fine, rake it level, and remove any large stones at the same time.

4 Most vegetables grown in rows, such as beetroots and carrots, are best sown in drills. Always use a garden line to make sure the drills – and therefore the rows – are straight.

5 Take out a shallow drill with the corner of a hoe or rake. Always refer to the seed packet for the recommended depth.

6 Flood the drills with water a few minutes before sowing if the weather is dry. Do it before sowing rather than after so that the seeds are not washed away or into clumps.

7 Sprinkle the seeds thinly and evenly along the drill. Do this carefully now and you will save time later when you would have to thin the seedlings if they come up too quickly.

8 Remove the garden line, then use your feet to shuffle the excavated soil back into the drills as you walk along the row. This technique is easy to master.

9 Use a rake to return soil to the drills if you find it easier, but rake in the direction of the row and not across it, otherwise you might spread the seeds and produce an uneven row.

FLUID SOWING

Fluid sowing is a technique some gardeners use to get the more difficult seeds off to a flying start. Parsnips, early carrots, onions and parsley are among the vegetables sometimes sown this way.

1 Sow the seeds thickly on damp kitchen paper, and keep in a warm place to germinate. Make sure that they remain moist, and check daily to monitor germination.

2 Once the roots emerge, and before the leaves open, wash the seeds into a sieve and mix them into prepared wallpaper paste (no fungicide) or a special sowing gel.

BELOW: *Carrots benefit from even sowing. The onions are to deter carrot fly!*

3 Take out the drill in the normal way, and to the usual depth.

4 Fill a plastic bag with the paste and cut off one corner (rather like an icing bag). Don't make the hole too large. Twist the top of the bag to prevent the paste oozing out, then move along the row as you squeeze out the seeds in the paste.

USING PREPARED SOWING STRIPS

From time to time strips of pre-sown seeds, embedded in a degradable material, may be available. These are an expensive way to buy seeds, but save much time and energy normally spent on spacing and thinning.

Take out a drill as advised and place the strip on edge in the drill. Return the soil to the drill, and keep the ground moist.

Because the seeds receive protection from the material in which they are embedded, and this sometimes also contains nutrients to give the seedlings a boost, you may find it an easy way to achieve a row of well-spaced seedlings.

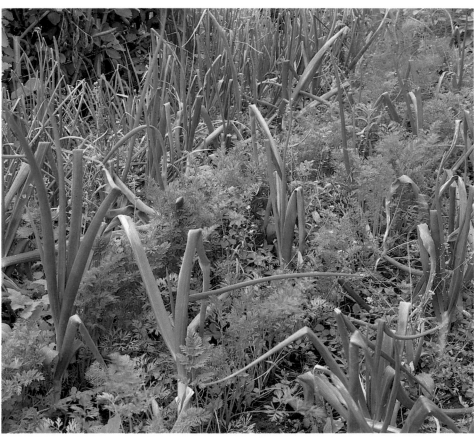

PLANT POTATOES

It is safe to plant potatoes in most areas, as it will take several weeks before the frost-sensitive shoots emerge from the soil, and these can be protected by earthing up the plants. In cold areas, however, it is best to chit your potatoes (see below) and delay planting for a couple of weeks. The use of cloches, floating cloches or fleece is wise in areas where frost is still likely.

1 Use a draw hoe, spade or a rake head to make wide, flat-bottomed or V-shaped drills 10–13cm (4–5in) deep. Space the rows about 43cm (17in) apart for early varieties, 68cm (2¼ft) for second earlies, and 75cm (2½ft) for the maincrop.

2 Space the tubers about 30–45cm (12–18in) apart in the rows. Make sure that the shoots or 'eyes' (buds about to grow into shoots) face upwards. For larger tubers, leave only three sprouts per plant and rub the others off.

CHITTING POTATO TUBERS

Chitting simply means encouraging the potato tubers to sprout before planting. The kind of long shoots that appear when potatoes have been stored in the dark for some time are no use – the shoots must be short and sturdy. Place the tubers in a tray in a light position, perhaps by a window, where there is no risk of frost.

Chitting is useful if you want the tubers to get off to a quick start, as they will usually be through the ground a week or two before unchitted tubers.

3 Cover the tubers by pulling the excavated soil back into the drill.

4 If you don't want the effort of earthing up your potatoes, plant under a black plastic sheet. Bury the edges in slits in the soil and cover with soil to anchor the sheet.

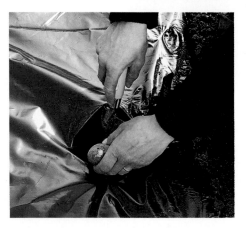

5 Make cross-shaped slits in the plastic with a knife where each tuber is to be planted.

6 Plant through the slit, using a trowel. Make sure that the tuber is covered with 3–5cm (1–2in) of soil. The shoots will find their way through the slits.

PLANT CABBAGES AND CAULIFLOWERS

Cabbages and cauliflowers are not normally sown in their final positions, but started off in seed beds, or sown in late winter and spring in pots or modules in the greenhouse, then transplanted to their growing positions. Buy young plants if you forgot to sow your own.

1 If you have your own seedlings to transplant into the vegetable patch – perhaps growing in a cold frame – water thoroughly an hour before you lift them if the soil is dry.

2 Loosen the soil with a fork or trowel. It is best to lift each one individually with a trowel if possible, but if they have not been thinned sufficiently this may be difficult.

PROTECTION FOR EARLY STRAWBERRIES

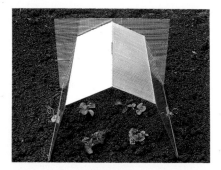

Strawberries do not need protection from frost, but cloches will bring the crop on earlier and will also help to keep it clean and protect it from birds and other animals.

Cover the plants as soon as possible, but remember to leave access for pollinating insects when the plants are in flower. Most cloches have a system of ventilation that can be used for this on warm days. With polythene tunnel cloches, lift the material along one side to allow for pollination.

3 Plant with a trowel and firm the soil well. A convenient way to firm soil around the roots is to insert the blade of the trowel about 5cm (2in) away from the plant and press it firmly towards the roots.

4 You can also firm the soil with the handle of the trowel if you don't want to use your hands, but this is not a good idea if the soil is wet as it will dirty the handle. Always water in thoroughly after transplanting.

5 Cabbage and cauliflower seedlings are often raised in modules so that the plants receive less of a shock when transplanted. Many modules are designed so that you can remove the plant by squeezing the base while gently pulling the plant at the top.

ABOVE: *Space cabbages as advised on the packet, as size varies.*

HOW TO MAKE A HERB WHEEL

If you have an old cartwheel, just paint or varnish that and set it into the ground ready to plant. Few of us have access to cartwheels, however, but an acceptable second best can be made from bricks. Adjust the size of the wheel to suit your garden. Bricks are a convenient way to make the 'spokes', but you could use dwarf dividing 'hedges' of hyssop or thyme. Place an attractive terracotta pot in the centre as the hub of the wheel, and plant with herbs, or place an upright rosemary in the centre. A rosemary may become too large after a few years, but either keep it clipped to shape and size or replace it every second or third year.

1 Mark a circle about 1.5–1.8m (5–6ft) across, using a line fixed to a peg to ensure an even shape. If it helps, use a wine bottle filled with dry sand instead of a stick to mark out the perimeter. Excavate the ground to a depth of about 15cm (6in).

2 Place the bricks on end, or at an angle, around the edge. If you place them at a 45 degree angle it will create a dog-tooth effect; bricks placed on end will look more formal. Either lay them loose in compacted earth, or bed them on mortar.

3 Lay rows of brick, cross-fashion, as shown. If the diameter does not allow for them to be laid without gaps in the centre, stand an ornament or pot in the middle if you are not planting directly into the soil in that position.

4 Top up the areas between the spokes with good garden or potting soil.

5 Plant up each section, using plants that will balance each other in size of growth if possible. You could, for instance, grow a collection of different thymes.

6 For a smart finish, carefully cover the soil with fine gravel.

SOW TENDER VEGETABLES

Mid spring is a good time to sow frost-tender vegetables in most areas. If they are sown too early they may be ready to plant out too soon, and they will start to suffer if they are kept in small containers for too long. Vegetables sown now should be ready for planting outdoors after a few weeks of growth in warmth followed by a week or so of acclimatization in a cold frame. In reasonably warm climates all the vegetables mentioned here can be sown outside once the risk of frost has passed. It is only worth sowing indoors if you want an early crop.

1 Sow runner beans about six to eight weeks before the last frost is likely. Fill a 15–20cm (6–8in) pot with sowing compost to within 3cm (1in) of the rim. Put three seeds in the pot, cover with about 2cm (3/4 in) of compost (soil mix) and water.

2 Keep the pots in a warm place, and give them good light as soon as the seeds germinate. If all the seeds germinate, pull out the surplus to leave just one or two seedlings.

3 Outdoor and greenhouse cucumbers can be sown now. Use small pots and fill with a seed-sowing mixture to within 3cm (1in) of the rim. Position two or three seeds in each pot, placing them on their narrow edge, cover with compost and water.

4 Keep the pots moist and warm until the seeds germinate. If more than one germinates, thin them at an early stage to leave just one seedling in each pot.

5 Marrows and courgettes can also be started off in pots. Treat like cucumbers, but as the seeds are larger use a bigger pot and plant about 3cm (1in) deep.

6 Sweet corn is best raised in pots to plant out later, except in very mild regions. You can use ordinary pots, but many gardeners prefer to use peat pots. The roots will grow through these once they are planted out. Peat pots are easier to manage if stood in a seed tray lined with a piece of capillary matting.

LATE SPRING

LATE SPRING CAN BE DECEPTIVE. It can seem as if summer has already arrived, yet in cold areas there can be severe late frosts. Take local climate into account before planting outdoors. A good guide is to watch when summer bedding is put out in the local parks, as these gardeners have amassed generations of local knowledge.

JOBS IN BRIEF

The Kitchen Garden

- ❑ Plant up a herb pot
- ❑ Begin to grow mints by trying out a collection in a growing bag
- ❑ Apply manures and fertilizers where appropriate
- ❑ Sow sweet corn and summer radishes outdoors in mild areas
- ❑ Sow vegetables without protection. Many kinds can be sown now, so check the packets
- ❑ Plant potatoes
- ❑ Plant out vegetable seedlings such as cabbages and cauliflowers
- ❑ Sow seeds of crops such as cabbages, cauliflowers and sprouts in a nursery bed, where they can be grown for transplanting later
- ❑ Put straw down around strawberries or protect with strawberry mats
- ❑ Sow or plant runner or pole beans outdoors

The Greenhouse and Conservatory

- ❑ Sow tender vegetables such as outdoor tomatoes and runner beans to plant out later
- ❑ Plant greenhouse tomatoes and cucumbers

TOP LEFT: *Plant out cabbage seedlings when the weather is moist and mild.*

TOP RIGHT: *In smaller gardens you can grow a selection of herbs in containers.*

RIGHT: *As an alternative to a cloche, use bundles of straw to protect strawberries during cold spells.*

CROPS IN SEASON

❑ **Asparagus** (for details on harvesting, see mid spring).

❑ **Chard** (for details on harvesting, see late summer).

❑ **Lettuces** grown outdoors or with the aid of a cloche can be harvested now. Harvest loose-leaf types a few leaves at a time.

❑ **Peas** Pick the pods as soon as the peas have swollen and are large enough to eat. Mangetout (snow peas) and similar types should be picked before the pods get tough. Keep picking the peas as they mature. The peas of many modern varieties, which have been created for agricultural needs, mature at the same time and this can be a problem for the gardener.

❑ **Summer Radishes** (for details on harvesting, see mid spring).

❑ **Rhubarb** (for details on harvesting, see mid spring).

❑ **Spinach** start harvesting as soon as the leaves are big enough, which is usually 8–12 weeks after sowing. Don't strip the plant; break or cut the stems, and try to avoid pulling because this may loosen the plant and precipitate bolting. Spinach can be harvested until the plants run to seed.

❑ **Turnips** can be harvested at this time of year. Pull up when the roots are about the size of a golf ball. You can check by scratching away soil from the top of the roots.

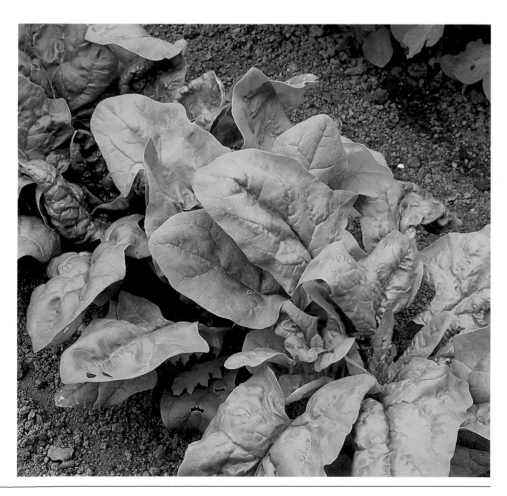

TOP LEFT: *Peas planted in a container.*

TOP RIGHT: *Harvesting turnips.*

BOTTOM RIGHT: *Rows of spinach.*

PLANT UP A HERB POT

A herb pot makes an attractive feature, but it is best treated as a short-term home to be replanted annually. If you allow shrubby perennial herbs to become large and established, you will find them extremely difficult to remove when it becomes necessary. Be especially careful of planting a large shrubby plant in the top of a herb pot with a tapering neck. Once the plant has produced a mass of roots, the inward taper makes removal a frustrating task.

1 A herb pot is best filled in stages. Start by adding a good potting compost to the height of the first planting pockets.

2 Using small plants, knock them out of their pots and push the root-balls through the holes in the planting pockets. If necessary, break off some of the root-ball so that you can get it through the hole.

3 Add more potting soil and repeat with the next row of planting holes. Unless the pot is very large, don't try to pack too many herbs into the top. A single well-grown plant often looks much better.

4 Large earthernware pots can look just as good as herb pots with planting pockets if you plant them imaginatively. If you have an old half-barrel use this instead. Place a bold shrubby herb, such as a sweet bay (*Laurus nobilis*), in the centre.

5 In time the shrubby plant may take up all the planting space at the top and you will have an attractive specimen plant, but meanwhile you should be able to fit a collection of smaller herbs around the edge. Avoid mints, which may be difficult to eliminate later.

GROW MINTS

Mints are notoriously difficult to control once they make themselves at home. They send spreading and penetrating shoots beneath the surface which emerge among other plants or even the other side of a path. They are best contained in some way.

1 A growing bag is an ideal home for mints. They will be happy for a couple of seasons, and then are easily removed and replanted for a fresh start. If the mints are in large pots it may be necessary to remove some of the root-ball, but they soon recover.

2 Instead of filling the growing bag with one kind of mint, try planting a collection of perhaps four to six different kinds. This will look good and add to the flavours available for the kitchen.

3 If you want to plant your mint in the border (which avoids the chore of watering frequently), plant it in an old bucket or large pot. Make sure that there are drainage holes in the bottom, and fill with soil or a potting mixture and plant the mint.

4 For a visually pleasing effect, position the rim of the pot just below the level of the surrounding soil, then cover with soil to hide any signs of the pot. Lift, divide and replant annually or every second spring, to maintain vigour.

OTHER HERBS TO RESTRAIN

Although mint is the herb most notorious for being invasive, others can attempt a take-over of the border. Tansy (*Tanacetum vulgare*) and woodruff (*Asperula odorata* syn. *Galium odoratum*) are among the herbs that you may also want to consider planting in a plunged bucket or large pot.

SOW SWEET CORN

Sweet corn is a reliable crop in warm areas, where it can be sown directly into the ground with confidence, but in cold regions with a short growing season, it is best to start the plants off under glass so that they have time to mature before the autumn frosts. In areas where growing conditions are less than favourable, choose a variety specially bred for a cool climate.

1 Sow only when there is no risk of frost and the soil temperature has reached 10°C (50°F). In cold areas, warm up the soil with fleece or cloches for a week or two first.

2 Sow the seeds 3cm (1in) deep and 8cm (3in) apart, and thin to the final recommended spacing later – typically 30cm (12in) apart each way. Sow in blocks rather than single rows.

3 Cover with a fine net floating cloche or horticultural fleece. This can be left on after germination until the plants have pushed the cover up to its limit without damaging the plants.

4 In areas where outdoor sowing is unreliable, raise the plants in modules or peat pots. Plant them out when there is no danger of frost, and after careful hardening off.

PLANT OUTDOOR TOMATOES

Wait until there is little risk of frost before planting your outdoor tomatoes – about the same time as you plant your tender summer bedding. Choose varieties recommended for outdoors.

1 Plant at the spacing recommended for the variety – some grow tall and large, others remain small and compact. Always make sure they have been well hardened off.

2 In cold areas, cover plants with cloches for a few weeks, or use horticultural fleece.

3 Once the fleece or protection has been removed, stake the plants immediately. Some small varieties may not require staking.

RAISING TOMATOES IN GROWING BAGS

Tomatoes do well in growing bags, and this is a practical way to grow them on a patio as well as in a greenhouse or vegetable patch.

Staking is the main problem if you want to grow tomatoes in growing bags on a hard base. There are many proprietary designs of cane supports intended for crops like tomatoes in growing bags, and most should last for several years.

If the growing bag is positioned on soil, you can simply push the cane through the bag, as shown.

PLANT RUNNER AND POLE BEANS

In mild areas runner and climbing French beans can be sown in late spring, but in cold areas wait until early summer or start the seeds off indoors. Do not plant out until there is no risk of frost.

1 Sow two seeds 5cm (2in) deep by each cane or support. Thin to one plant later if both germinate. Wait until the soil temperature is at least 12°C (54°F) before sowing.

2 If you raised the plants in pots, plant out once there is no reasonable risk of frost. Use a trowel and plant them just outside the cane. Train them to the cane as soon as they are tall enough.

SUPPORTING RUNNER AND POLE BEANS

Canes and nets are the main methods of supporting runner and pole beans. If you use a net, choose a large-mesh net sold as a pea and bean net, and stretch it taut between well-secured posts. If you use canes, the most popular methods are wigwams (see right) and crossed canes (see far right).

Proprietary supports are also available but, although usually very effective, they can be expensive.

PLANT GREENHOUSE TOMATOES

Greenhouse tomatoes always used to be grown in the greenhouse border, and the soil changed periodically. This was considered risky and ring culture became fashionable. In more recent times growing bags have been in favour. Other methods are used commercially but the three

practical and easy methods suitable for amateurs are described here. All three systems have merits and drawbacks, and how well you look after your tomatoes while they are growing can be as important as the system. Choose the one that appeals most or seems the easiest.

1 Always dig in as much rotted manure or garden compost as you can spare and rake in a general garden fertilizer before you plant your tomatoes. Although they can be planted earlier, most amateurs find this is a good time as the greenhouse usually has more space once the bedding plants have been moved out.

2 Most greenhouse varieties grow tall and need support. Tall canes are a convenient method if you have just a few plants, but if you have a lot of plants the string method may be more suitable (see opposite).

3 With ring culture, the water-absorbing roots grow into a moist aggregate and the feeding roots into special bottomless pots filled with a potting compost. Take out a trench about 15–23cm (6–9in) deep in the greenhouse border and line it with a waterproof plastic (this minimizes soil-borne disease contamination).

4 Fill the trench with fine gravel, coarse grit or expanded clay granules. Then place the special bottomless ring culture pots on the aggregate base and fill them with a good potting compost.

5 Plant into the ring and insert a cane or provide an alternative support. Water only into the ring at first. Once the plant is established and some roots have penetrated into the aggregate, water only the aggregate and feed through the pot.

6 Growing bags are less trouble than ring culture to set up, but you still have to feed plants regularly, and watering can be more difficult to control unless you use an automatic system. Insert a cane through the bag or use a string support.

ABOVE: *You can expect crops like this if you plant your greenhouse tomatoes now. For best results, check that the variety is recommended for greenhouse cultivation.*

SUPPORTING TOMATOES ON STRINGS

String is a simple and economical way to support your tomatoes. Fix one wire as high as practical from one end of the greenhouse to the other, aligning it above the border, and another one just above the ground. The lower wire is most conveniently fixed to a stout stake at each end of the row.

Tie lengths of string between the top and bottom wires, in line with each plant.

You don't need to tie the plant to its support, just loop the string around the growing tip so that it forms a spiral.

PLANT AND TRAIN CUCUMBERS

As with tomatoes, there are various ways to plant and train cucumbers.

Try growing cucumbers in growing bags on the greenhouse staging. Insert canes between the growing bags and the eaves, and fix horizontal wires along the length of the roof as shown here. You can then train the growth along the roof and the cucumbers will hang down. A normal growing bag should hold about two cucumbers. Do not over-crowd the plants.

The method shown is easy and convenient, but if you don't want the trouble of ensuring that the growing bags are kept evenly moist, you could plant the cucumbers directly into the border soil and start the horizontal wires on the sides of the greenhouse instead.

SUMMER

Summer is a time when the kitchen gardener can begin to enjoy the fruits of his or her labours. Crops such as cauliflowers, radishes and peppers can be enjoyed at this time, and as summer begins to dwindle, many fruits such as apples and pears will be ripening. There is still much work to be done during the summer. To keep the kitchen garden productive in autumn and winter, continue to sow suitable vegetables, and keep an ever vigilant eye out for pests which like nothing better than to feast on your crops before you get a chance to bring them to the kitchen table. Now is also the time to pick and preserve fruit and vegetables to enjoy in winter.

ABOVE: *A box-edged potager combines plantings of vegetables and flowers.*

OPPOSITE: *Apples trained in an arch make a decorative feature.*

EARLY SUMMER

EARLY SUMMER IS A TIME when you can relax a little and enjoy your efforts of the past months. But there are still jobs to be done. Crops such as sweet corn need to be sown to ensure a winter harvest, and pests and diseases are as active as ever. Vigilance and prompt action now will often stop the trouble from spreading out of control.

JOBS IN BRIEF

The Kitchen Garden

❑ Sow sweet corn outdoors in mild areas when further frost is unlikely
❑ Sow vegetables, following the details given on seed packets
❑ Make successional sowings of crops such as beetroot, carrots, lettuces and turnips
❑ Plant potatoes
❑ Plant out vegetable seedlings such as cabbages, cauliflowers, celery, sweet corn, and tomatoes
❑ Sow in a nursery bed seeds of crops such as cabbages, sprouts and cauliflowers, where they can be grown for later transplanting
❑ Protect and earth up potatoes planted earlier in the year
❑ Sow French (green) beans
❑ Sow or plant runner and pole beans outdoors
❑ Watch out for aphids on broad beans and root flies on cabbages, carrots and onions

The Greenhouse and Conservatory

❑ Try biological pest control for pests
❑ Start to feed tomatoes when the first truss has set. Remove side-shoots and yellow leaves regularly

TOP LEFT: *When transplanting a seedling, lift with as much soil as possible around the roots.*

TOP RIGHT: *Aphids can ruin crops if left unchecked.*

RIGHT: *Early summer is a good time to start earthing up potatoes.*

CROPS IN SEASON

- **Asparagus** (for details on harvesting, see mid spring).
- **Beetroot (beets)** Pull the young beetroot from the ground while still quite small. This will be about seven weeks after sowing. If possible, do not break the thin root attached to the bottom of the globe because this will "bleed" causing the beetroot (beet) to lose alot of its colour.
- **Broad (fava) beans** Pick the pods when they are about the size of your little finger and the beans inside them have swollen. Do not allow the beans to become too old. Broad beans can also be picked or eaten whole.
- **Mangetout** Pick mangetout while the peas are visible only as tiny swellings. When the crop has finished, chop off the stems leaving the roots in the ground. This will help to enrich the soil.
- **Peas** (for details on how to harvest, see late summer).
- **Summer radishes** (for details on harvesting, see mid spring).
- **Rhubarb** (for details on harvesting, see mid spring).
- **Shallots** can be harvested now. Harvest in the same way as onions
- **Spinach** (for details on harvesting, see late spring and mid autumn).
- **Turnips** (for advice on harvesting, see late spring and mid autumn).

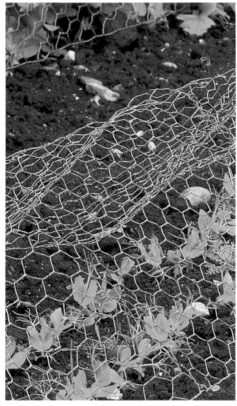

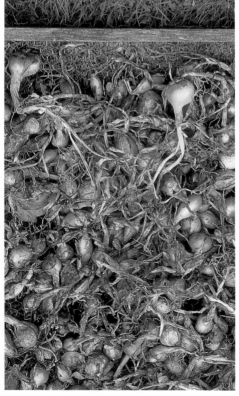

TOP LEFT: *Rows of spinach.*

TOP RIGHT: *Chicken wire provides protection for peas.*

BOTTOM LEFT: *Harvesting beetroot (beets).*

BOTTOM RIGHT: *Shallots drying in the sunshine.*

PROTECT AND EARTH UP POTATOES

Potatoes are earthed up to protect the tubers near the surface from light. If they are exposed, their skins will turn green and the tubers will be completely inedible.

1 Potatoes will usually recover from slight frost damage, but if you know that a frost is forecast once the shoots are through the ground, try covering the plants with newspaper or horticultural fleece. Peg into position, then remove the next morning or when the frost has gone.

2 Start earthing up the potatoes when the shoots are about 15cm (6in) high. Use a draw hoe to pull up the soil either side of the row.

3 Continue to earth up in stages, as the potatoes grow, until the soil creates a mound about 15cm (6in) high.

THIN SEEDLINGS

Thinning is a tedious but essential task. The final spacing between plants will determine both the size of the individual vegetables and the total yield. Exact spacing will often depend on whether you are more interested in the total crop or large, well-shaped individual specimens.

1 Follow the spacing advice given on the seed packet when sowing. It should also recommend the ideal final spacing between plants after thinning.

2 Thin in stages, pulling up surplus plants between finger and thumb. The first thinning should leave the plants twice as close as their final spacing, to allow for losses after thinning.

3 Before the plants begin to compete with each other, thin once more to the final spacing.

SOWING MINI-CAULIFLOWERS

Mini-cauliflowers are summer varieties sown in spring or early summer but grown at much closer spacing than normal. Sow several seeds every 15cm (6in) where they are to grow, and thin these to one seedling if more than one germinates. The heads are much smaller than normal, but total yield can still be good.

MULTIPLE SOWING

TRANSPLANTING SEEDLINGS

Do not attempt to transplant spare thinnings of root crops such as carrots and turnips, but other crops – like lettuces and cabbages, for example – can transplant satisfactorily.

The secret of success is to water the row thoroughly an hour before you thin or transplant (check to make sure that moisture has penetrated to root level), and to lift the spare seedlings with as much soil as possible around the roots. Always water well until plants recover, and shade from direct sun for a few days.

Some gardeners grow certain vegetables – such as carrots, beetroot, onions and leeks, in small clusters. Four to six seeds are usually sown in each cell of modular trays (see top), and planted out without any attempt to separate them. These are not normally thinned. The vegetables are usually smaller and less well shaped than those sown in rows and thinned normally, but the overall weight of crop may be good if the spacing recommended for this type of cultivation is followed (see above).

LEFT: *The total yield can sometimes be higher from close spacing, even though individual specimens are smaller.*

MID SUMMER

MID SUMMER IS MAINLY A TIME to enjoy your garden, rather than do a lot of physical work in it. Most things are already sown or planted, and the emphasis is on weeding and watering. Continue to thin vegetables, sow crops such as winter cabbages and leeks and, of course, remain ever aware of the damage pests can do.

JOBS IN BRIEF

The Kitchen Garden

❑ Hoe regularly to keep down weeds

❑ Sow more vegetables including spinach, parsley, winter radishes and (in cold areas) spring cabbage. Make successional sowings of crops such as beetroot (beets), carrots, lettuces and turnips

❑ Continue to thin vegetables sown earlier, before they start competing with each other

❑ Plant out late cauliflowers, winter cabbages and leeks

❑ Sow more French (green) beans

❑ Give plants that need a boost a dressing dose of quick-acting fertilizer, but if using a powder or granules, water thoroughly

❑ Pinch out the growing tips of runner beans when they reach the top of their support

❑ Lift shallots if they have finished growing, and leave them on the surface for a few days to dry off

❑ Harvest herbs regularly. Don't let the leaves become too old

❑ Thin apples

❑ Summer prune cordon and espalier apples

❑ Water vulnerable crops before they show signs of stress

❑ Tidy up summer-flowering strawberries that have finished fruiting. Cut off old leaves and unwanted runners, remove straw, and control weeds

❑ Remain vigilant for early signs of pests and diseases. Caterpillars can devastate a cabbage crop

The Greenhouse and Conservatory

❑ Feed tomatoes regularly and remove sideshoots and any yellowing leaves

❑ Keep a vigilant watch for pests and diseases. Spray promptly or try a biological control for greenhouse pests

TOP: *Hoeing weeds with a cultivator.*

RIGHT: *Mints growing in containers. Mints are invasive, so this is a perfect way of keeping them under control.*

CROPS IN SEASON

❏ **Beetroot (beets)** (for details on harvesting, see early summer).

❏ **Black, red and white currants** Pick the fruit as it ripens, taking the whole cluster of fruit and retaining the stalks. They can be frozen or turned into preserves.

❏ **Broad (fava) beans** (for details on harvesting, see early summer).

❏ **Carrots** Harvesting can begin at a very early stage as the thinnings can be delicious, although they are rather tedious to clean. If your garden has a light soil, leave them in the ground and pull as required, if not then store carrots in boxes of sand for protection.

❏ **Courgettes and marrows (zucchini)** can be picked now. Pick courgettes regularly to keep plants cropping. If you are after a record-breaking marrow, pick off all the fruit except for one.

❏ **Cucumbers** Cut the fruit with a short length of stalk as soon as they are large enough to eat. Harvest gherkins when 5–8cm/ 2–3in long.

❏ **French (green) beans** are picked while still young and the pods snap cleanly in half. Repeat every 2–3 days for the 6–8 week lifespan of the crop. Picking regularly encourages more to form. When the crop is over, chop off stems but leave roots in the ground. This will have a beneficial effect on the soil.

❏ **Mangetout** (for details on harvesting, see early summer).

❏ **Onions** are ready to harvest when the foilage starts to wither. Dry if you plan to store them.

❏ **Pears** should be picked as soon as the fruit comes away readily

BELOW: *Picking runner beans.*

BELOW: *Cordon pears ready to be harvested.*

BELOW: *Harvesting tomatoes.*

with a slight twisting of the hand. Early varieties can be picked just before they ripen, but mid-season and late varieties should be left until ripe.

❏ **Summer radishes** (for details on harvesting, see mid spring).

❏ **Raspberries and strawberries** both have been developed so that it is possible to have a supply of fruit from summer right through to the first frosts. Harvest as fruit ripens.

❏ **Rhubarb** (for details on harvesting see mid spring).

❏ **Runner beans** Pick the pods before the beans have started to swell inside. If you leave mature pods on the plants, they will not feel inclined to produce more.

❏ **Shallots** (for details on harvesting, see early summer).

❏ **Tomatoes** come into season now. For the best flavour, leave the fruit to ripen fully on the plant.

❏ **Turnips** (for details on harvesting, see late spring and mid autumn).

CONTROL WEEDS

It is never possible to eliminate weeds entirely, but you can control them. Even weeds that are difficult to eradicate can be conquered if you persist, and annual weeds will diminish in numbers if you continue to kill off the seedlings before they can flower and shed more seed.

Once the weed population has been reduced, mulching and prompt action to remove the seedlings that do appear will keep the garden almost weed-free. Be prepared for the battle to be won over a couple of seasons rather than in a few weeks if the garden has been neglected.

1 Deep-rooted perennial weeds that have long, penetrating roots are best forked up. Loosen the roots with a fork, and hold the stem close to its base as you pull up the whole plant. If you don't get all the root out, new pieces may grow.

2 Hoeing is one of the best forms of weed control, but it needs to be done regularly. Slice the weeds off just beneath the soil, preferably when the soil is dry. Keep beds and borders hoed, as well as the vegetable garden.

3 Contact chemical weedkillers are useful if you need to clear an area of ground quickly and easily. Some – which normally only kill the top growth, so are better for annuals than problem perennial weeds – leave the area safe to replant after a day.

4 Some weedkillers kill the whole plant, including the roots. Large areas of ground can be sprayed, but you can paint some formulations onto the leaves to kill the weed without harming neighbouring plants.

5 Mulches are very effective at controlling weeds. In the vegetable and fruit garden various forms of plastic sheeting are a cost-effective method.

6 Where appearance matters, use an organic material such as chipped bark, garden compost or cocoa shells. If the ground is cleared of weeds first, a mulch at least 5cm (2in) thick will suppress most weeds.

SUMMER PRUNE CORDON AND ESPALIER APPLES

Shaped and trained apple trees are normally pruned twice a year – once in summer and again in winter. Summer pruning controls the amount of growth produced each year and maintains the basic shape, winter pruning consists of thinning overcrowded fruiting spurs on old plants. In late spring the new growth at the ends of the main shoots is cut back to its point of origin, but summer pruning is the most crucial in terms of maintaining the trained shape.

ESPALIER

1 Shorten new leafy shoots that have grown directly from the main branches back to three leaves above the basal cluster of leaves. This should only be done once the shoots have dark green leaves and the bark has started to turn brown and is woody at the base. In cold areas it may be early autumn before the shoots are mature enough.

2 If the shoot is growing from a stub left by previous pruning – and not directly from one of the main stems – cut back to just one leaf above the basal cluster of leaves.

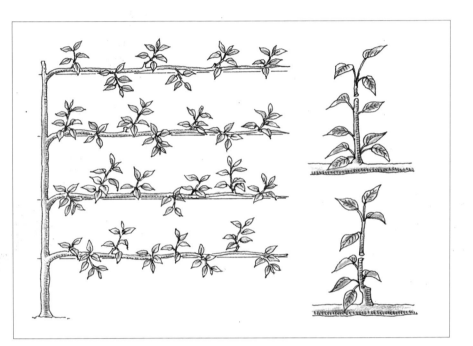

CORDON

1 A cordon is pruned in exactly the same way as an espalier, although, of course, the basic shape of the plant is different. Just cut back shoots growing directly from the main branch to three leaves above the basal cluster of leaves.

2 Cut back shoots growing from stubs left by earlier pruning to one leaf above the basal cluster.

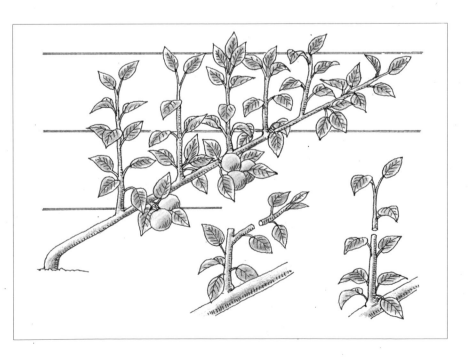

SUMMER CARE FOR GREENHOUSE TOMATOES

The varieties of tomato usually grown in the greenhouse need regular attention, like the removal of sideshoots, feeding, and tying in.

Keep a watch too for early signs of pests and diseases that could otherwise reduce the quantity or quality of the crop.

1 If the plants are supported by strings, simply loop the string around the top of the shoot whenever necessary. It will form a spiral support that holds the stem upright.

2 To secure the plant to a cane, wrap the string twice around the stake and then loop it loosely around the stem before tying the knot.

3 Snap off sideshoots while they are still small. They will snap off cleanly if you pull them sideways. Do not remove sideshoots if you have a low-growing bush variety.

4 If fruits are failing to form, poor pollination may be the problem. Shake the plants each day, or spray the flowers with water, to spread the pollen.

5 The lowest leaves often turn yellow as they age. Remove these, as they will not contribute to feeding the plant, and letting more light reach the fruits can help to ripen them.

6 'Stop' your plants, by removing the growing tip, when they have formed as many trusses of fruit as are likely to ripen. In an unheated greenhouse this may be as few as four in cold areas; six or seven in warmer regions.

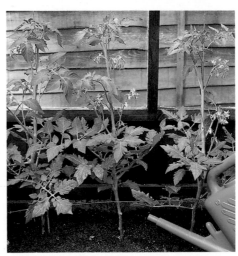

7 Tomatoes respond well to feeding. Some tomato feeds are high in nitrogen for early growth, but now that the fruit is developing, a high-potash tomato fertilizer is best.

OTHER GREENHOUSE CROPS

Greenhouse crops like aubergines, cucumbers and melons also need attention at this time of year if you want to ensure a good, healthy crop.

CARING FOR MELONS

Train the sideshoot of melons to horizontal wires, and pinch back the sideshoots to two leaves beyond each fruit that develops. Melons may require pollinating, in which case transfer the pollen from the male to female flowers with a small paintbrush. It may also be necessary to support developing fruits with nets, as shown.

1 Aubergines make bushier plants if the growing tip is pinched out when the plant is about 30cm (12in) high. Allow only one fruit to develop on each shoot. Pinch out the growing tips of these shoots three leaves beyond the developing fruit. Never let the plants dry out, and feed regularly. Regular misting to provide high humidity is beneficial.

2 Many modern cucumbers produce only female flowers, but there are some varieties you might grow in a greenhouse that produce both male and female blooms (the female flowers have a small embryo fruit behind the petals). Pinch out male flowers before they have a chance to pollinate the female ones, as this can make the cucumbers less palatable.

DAMPING DOWN

Splashing or spraying water over the greenhouse path (traditionally known as damping down) helps to create a humid atmosphere. This is especially beneficial for crops such as aubergines and cucumbers, but most plants appreciate a moist atmosphere on a hot day – including the majority of pot-plants. Do it frequently on very hot days, to create the kind of hot and humid atmosphere that most tropical plants prefer.

LATE SUMMER

LATE SUMMER IS USUALLY A TIME of hot, dry weather, when there is a natural lull in the garden and the efforts of spring and early summer sowing and planting have paid dividends. The chores of autumn can wait for a while. Concentrate on watering, hoeing, pruning and weeding, and continue to thin vegetables where needed.

JOBS IN BRIEF

The Kitchen Garden

❑ Continue to hoe regularly to keep down weeds

❑ Lift onions and shallots as they become ready

❑ Continue to thin vegetables which were sown earlier

❑ Give plants that need a boost a dose of a quick-acting fertilizer

❑ Sow cabbages for spring use

❑ Pinch out the growing tips of runner beans when they reach the top of their support

❑ Pay regular attention to watering and feeding outdoor tomatoes

❑ Continue to harvest herbs regularly for a fresh supply of culinary seasonings

❑ Summer prune cordon and espalier apples if not already done so and shoots are mature enough

❑ Protect fruit against birds if they are a problem; a fruit cage is ideal

The Greenhouse and Conservatory

❑ Continue to feed tomatoes and to deal with routine tasks

❑ Keep a vigilant watch for pests and diseases

TOP LEFT: *Coriander (cilantro) is ready for harvesting now*

TOP RIGHT: *Courgettes (zucchini) are ready for harvesting in late summer*

RIGHT: *A traditional vegetable plot with two rows of tomatoes.*

AUTUMN

As summer begins to draw to a close, there is still much work to be done in the garden. Beware of the vagaries of the weather, and be prepared to protect less resilient crops during bouts of severe cold. Crops such as lettuces and other low-growing vegetables will continue to crop for longer with the protection of a cloche. Check that the greenhouse and its heaters are in working order, as autumn is the time that it shrugs off its supporting role to become a star player during the winter chill. If the garden has been managed properly during summer, it will remain productive throughout autumn. A plethora of other crops from the humble parsnip to the globe artichoke are also still in season. Fruits such as apples, pears and blackcurrants are at their best now, so pick and enjoy!

ABOVE: *A wonderful harvest makes all your hard work seem worthwhile.*

OPPOSITE: *Onions hanging out to dry in a traditional cottage garden.*

EARLY AUTUMN

THE WEATHER IN EARLY AUTUMN is still warm enough to make outdoor gardening a comfortable experience, and there is still much to do. Keep an eye on vulnerable crops and protect with cloches or alternative sheltering if necessary. Plenty of vegetables and fruit can still be harvested, including celery, sprouts, and swede.

JOBS IN BRIEF

The Kitchen Garden

❏ Lift onions to store
❏ Place cloches over lettuces and other low-growing vegetables that will continue to crop for longer with protection
❏ Sow a crop of a green manure (such as mustard) to use up nutrients in vacant ground, which will be recycled when dug in
❏ Lift and store maincrop potatoes
❏ Protect outdoor tomatoes with cloches or fleece to extend their season and ripen more fruit
❏ Summer prune cordon and espalier apples if not already done
❏ Clean and store canes and stakes that have supported crops

The Greenhouse and Conservatory

❏ Check that the greenhouse heaters are in good working order. Arrange to have them serviced, if necessary
❏ Ventilate the greenhouse if the weather is mild
❏ Vegetables such as lettuce can be grown indoors

TOP LEFT: *Potatoes will be coming into season at this time of year.*

TOP RIGHT: *Climbing French (green) beans can be supported with a bamboo cane. They can be harvested from mid summer until the first frosts.*

RIGHT: *Lamb's lettuce can be sown as a winter crop and does not need any protection.*

CROPS IN SEASON

- **Apples** (for details on harvesting, see late summer).
- **Aubergines (eggplants)** (for details on harvesting, see late summer).
- **Beetroot (beets)** (for details on harvesting, see early summer).
- **Broad (fava) beans** (for details on harvesting, see early summer).
- **Brussels sprouts** should be harvested when the sprouts are still large enough to pick but while they are still tight. Start at the bottom, moving up the stems as the sprouts fill out. When all are removed, pick the loose heads or tops and cook them as greens.
- **Carrots** (for details on harvesting, see mid summer).
- **Cauliflowers** (for details on harvesting, see late summer).
- **Celery** (for details on harvesting, see late summer).
- **Chard** (for details on harvesting, see late summer).
- **Courgettes and Marrows (zucchini)** (for details on harvesting, see mid summer).
- **Cucumbers** (for details on harvesting, see mid summer).
- **French (green) beans** (for details on harvesting, see mid summer).
- **Maincrop potatoes** are left in the soil until the autumn and are usually all lifted at once and stored. To harvest earlies, dig a fork in well below the potatoes and lever them out of the soil, at the same time pulling on the haulm (stems and leaves). For maincrop, remove the haulm about two weeks before harvesting so that the skins on the potatoes harden. Lift the maincrop on a sunny day and leave to dry.
- **Onions** (for details on harvesting, see mid summer).

BELOW: *Broad (fava) beans.*

BELOW: *Harvesting celery from a trench.*

BELOW: *Digging up potatoes.*

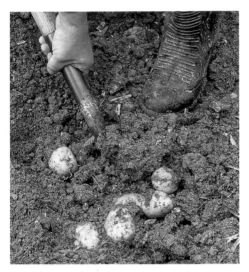

BELOW: *Apple 'Greensleeves' trained to shape.*

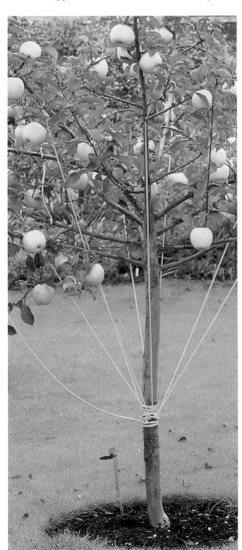

- **Peppers** (for details on harvesting, see late summer).
- **Strawberries and raspberries** these are still available to harvest. See mid summer for details.
- **Summer radishes** (for details on harvesting, see mid spring).
- **Swedes (yellow turnips)** Lift when they reach a usable size.
- **Sweet corn** (for details on harvesting, see late summer).
- **Tomatoes** (for details on harvesting, see mid summer).

PUT CLOCHES IN PLACE

If you have cloches that you normally use to protect your crops in spring, make the most of them by extending the end of the season as well as the beginning.

Save large barn cloches for large crops such as tomatoes (see opposite), if wished, and use tent and plastic tunnel cloches for low-growing crops such as lettuces.

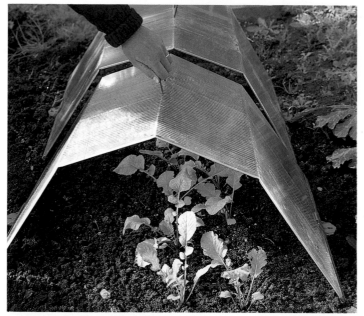

1 Winter radishes and mooli radishes are frost-hardy, but you can encourage further growth before bad weather sets in by covering them with cloches. If you failed to sow them earlier, you may be able to start them off under cloches now in a mild area, provided you do so while the soil is still warm.

2 Try sowing lamb's lettuce and winter purslane as a cold month crop. They don't need cloche protection except in cold areas, but the cover will ensure a better supply of more succulent leaves.

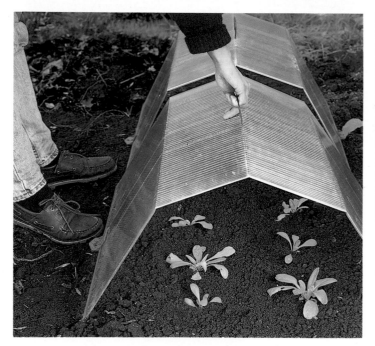

3 Put the cloches in position before the cold weather checks growth. With a little protection like this the plants will crop more freely.

ABOVE: *Put cloches in place now to warm up the soil for early crops such as lettuces.*

RIGHT: *Beetroot can also be sown earlier if you first warm the soil with cloches.*

PROTECT OUTDOOR TOMATOES

Green tomatoes can be ripened indoors provided they have reached a reasonable stage of maturity, but it makes sense to ripen as many as possible on the plant. As soon as a severe frost is forecast, however, harvest the remaining fruit and ripen as many as possible indoors.

1 Frost will kill tomatoes, but you can often extend their season by a few weeks and ripen a few more fruits on the plant with protection. Bush plants that are already low-growing are best covered with a large cloche. Packing straw beneath the plants first will also provide a little insulation.

2 Cordon-trained tomatoes must be lowered before they can be protected with cloches. Untie the plant and remove the stake.

3 Lay a bed of straw on the ground, then carefully lower the plants onto this. If you lay all the stems in the same direction, you will have a neat row of tomatoes that are easily covered with cloches.

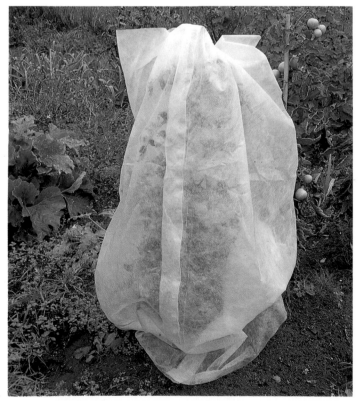

4 Fleece can be used to offer wind protection and enough shelter to keep off a degree or two of frost, though it does not warm the air during the day in the same way as glass or some rigid plastics. Drape several layers over low-growing varieties, and peg it down securely along each side, and at the ends.

5 Fleece can also be used to protect cordon tomatoes while still staked. Sheets of fleece can be wrapped round, or you may be able to buy fleece produced as a tube. Simply cut off the required length, slip it over the plant, and secure at the top and bottom.

MID AUTUMN

THIS IS AN UNPREDICTABLE TIME of the year. In cold regions quite severe frosts are not uncommon, while in mild climates, some plants are still growing. Listen to the weather forecast, watch other gardeners in the area, and above all, be flexible and ready to offer protection to crops vulnerable to the cold.

JOBS IN BRIEF

The Kitchen Garden

❏ Plant cabbages for harvesting in the spring

❏ Thin late-sown lettuces for harvesting in winter

❏ Continue to earth up celery and leeks to ensure a healthy crop

❏ Lift and store potatoes

❏ Protect late cauliflowers from frost by bending surrounding leaves over the heads

❏ Cut the dead tops off asparagus

❏ Use cloches to protect vulnerable vegetables from cold weather

❏ Start off the task of winter digging on heavy soils

❏ Pot up some herbs for using in winter dishes

❏ Pick and store apples when ready

❏ Take blackcurrant cuttings

❏ Prune blackcurrants, gooseberries and raspberries

❏ Cover late-fruiting strawberries with cloches in order to extend the season

❏ Plant bare-root fruit trees and bushes while they are dormant

❏ Apply greasebands to apple trees. This is a non-chemical method of controlling some fruit pests

The Greenhouse and Conservatory

❏ Clean, disinfect and insulate

❏ Remove yellowing and dead leaves from plants, picking them off the pot as well as the plant

❏ Check that heaters are in good working order

❏ Check minimum temperatures are being achieved (if you don't have a minimum-maximum thermometer, buy one)

❏ Ventilate whenever the weather is mild enough

TOP RIGHT: *Minimum-maximum thermometers can be used to check the temperature in the greenhouse or conservatory.*

RIGHT: *Victorian-type glass cloches are perfect for protecting vulnerable vegetables. These antique ones are obviously expensive, so opt for the cheaper plastic alternatives that are available.*

CROPS IN SEASON

- **Apples** (for details on harvesting, see late summer).
- **Aubergines (eggplants)** (for details on harvesting, see late summer).
- **Beetroot (beets)** (for details on harvesting, see early summer).
- **Brussels sprouts** (for details on harvesting, see early autumn).
- **Carrots** (for details on harvesting, see mid summer).
- **Cauliflowers** (for details on harvesting, see late summer).
- **Celeriac** This can be left in the ground, even in winter until needed.
- **Celery** (for details on harvesting, see late summer).
- **Chard** for details on harvesting, see late summer).
- **Courgettes and marrows (zucchini)** (for details on harvesting, see mid summer).
- **Cucumbers** (for details on harvesting, see mid summer).
- **French (green) beans** (for details on harvesting, see mid summer).
- **Leeks** can be lifted for use at any time between mid autumn and late spring. Dig them out with a fork. Autumn varieties are not as hardy – harvest before mid winter.
- **Maincrop potatoes** (for details on harvesting, see early autumn).
- **Parsnips** can be harvested from autumn onwards. Although they can be harvested before the leaves die back, most people wait for this.
- **Runner beans** (for details on harvesting, see mid summer).
- **Salsify and scorzonera** taste best after they have been exposed to a frost. Dig the roots up with a fork taking care not to bruise or damage them. **Salsify**

BELOW: *Harvesting parsnips.*

BELOW: *Salsify growing in clumps.*

BELOW: *Storing potatoes.*

BELOW: *Turnips ready for harvesting.*

should be harvested and used during the first winter because it is a biennial. **Scorzonera**, however, is a perennial and can be left in the ground and harvested in the following autumn and winter, which gives the roots a chance to get larger.

- **Peppers** (for details on harvesting, see late summer).
- **Spinach** Start harvesting as soon as the leaves are big enough, which is usually 8–12 weeks after sowing. Don't strip the plant; break or cut the stems, and try to avoid pulling because this may precipitate bolting. Harvest until the plant runs to seed.

- **Strawberries and raspberries** can still be enjoyed during the autumn months.
- **Swedes (yellow turnips)** (for details on harvesting, see early autumn).
- **Sweet corn** (for details on harvesting, see late summer).
- **Tomatoes** (for details on harvesting, see mid summer).
- **Turnips** can be harvested at this time of year. Pull up when the roots are about the size of a golf ball. You can check by scratching away soil from the top of the roots.
- **Winter radishes** should be eaten quickly before they become tough.

LIFT AND STORE POTATOES

Early and mid-season varieties are best eaten soon after harvesting, but the late varieties are grown mainly for storing for winter use. If you grow a small quantity they are best stored in paper sacks kept indoors, but if you grow a lot and indoor storage space is limited, try using the traditional clamping method. It looks primitive but works except where winters are very severe.

1 Lift the tubers with a fork once the foliage has died down. You can leave them in the ground for longer if penetrating frosts are not likely to be a problem, but lift promptly if pests like slugs appear.

2 Leave the potatoes on the surface for a couple of hours so that the skins dry off and harden.

3 Sort the potatoes before storing. It is sufficient to grade them into four sizes: very small, small, medium and large. Discard or use up very small ones immediately, keep small ones for use soon, and only store the medium and largest.

RIGHT: *Potatoes are best left to dry off for a couple of hours before sorting and storing.*

4 Place the largest potatoes in sacks to store in a cool but frost-proof place. Paper sacks are best, but if you can't obtain them, use plastic sacks in which case make slits with a knife to provide some ventilation.

5 If you have too many potatoes to store in sacks, or don't have space indoors, make a clamp in the garden. Excavate a shallow depression and line it with a thick layer of straw.

6 Pile the potatoes on to the bed of straw, as shown.

7 Heap a thick layer of straw over the top. It must be thick enough to provide good insulation.

8 Mound earth over the straw, but leave a few tufts of straw sticking out of the top for ventilation.

PROLONGING HERBS

Parsley is one of the herbs that will continue to provide leaves for harvesting throughout the winter if you protect the plants with cloches. Make sure that the end pieces are tightly secured.

STRAW PROTECTION

Vegetables such as celery (shown here) and beetroot benefit in cold areas if you protect the stems with straw. Pack the straw among and between the plants in the blocks or rows. It does not matter if the tops of the leaves are exposed – you are only protecting the edible part.

Mature celery will usually survive some frost, but the protection is useful if it turns very cold before you are ready to lift it. In mild areas you can leave beetroot unprotected, but the straw does help to keep plants in better condition for longer in cold areas.

INSULATE THE GREENHOUSE

Insulation will cut down heating costs. Even if you don't heat your greenhouse during the winter, insulation will afford extra protection for those not–quite–hardy plants.

1 There are many pro-prietary fasteners for securing polythene to the inside of a metal greenhouse. Details may vary, but they slot into the groove in the metal moulding and can be secured in position with a twisting motion.

2 With the main part of the clip in place, the top is pushed or twisted into position, clamping the polythene liner. If using thick bubble polythene, you may need to buy clips designed for the extra thickness.

3 You may find it easier to line the sides and roof separately. If you decide to do this, be prepared to use a draught proofing strip if there is a gap at the eaves.

4 You can fix the insulation to a timber-framed greenhouse with drawing pins, or special pins sold for the purpose.

5 If you don't want to fix the insulation directly to the wooden frame, suction fixers can be attached to the glass. These can also be used for metal-framed greenhouses. Moisten the plastic before pressing into place.

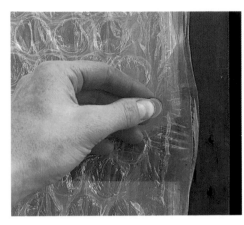

7 Whichever method of fixing you choose, you should always insulate the ventilators separately. Although you need to conserve heat as much as possible, some ventilation is essential when it's warm enough. You must be able to open at least one ventilator if necessary.

6 Secure the liner to the cup with the special pin provided (or use a drawing pin).

8 To avoid too much warmth being lost between the sheets where they join, seal joins with a transparent tape.

RIGHT: *Bubble insulation will keep the temperature up and your bills down.*

SCREENS AND DIVIDERS

Thermal screens made of clear plastic or special translucent fabrics are widely used commercially to conserve heat. Fixed horizontally over the plants, they seal off the space at the top of the greenhouse. They are usually pulled across at night, and drawn back during the day. A similar technique can be used in your own greenhouse by stretching supporting wires along each side of the greenhouse, over which the fabric can be draped or pulled (see below left).

If you have a large greenhouse, it may be more economic to heat just part of it. Use a vertical screen to partition off the end (see below right) to reduce the area to be heated.

INSULATION MATERIALS

Proper double glazing is not very practical or cost-effective for most amateur greenhouses where very high temperatures are not normally maintained. Polythene sheeting is the most practical choice as it can be taken down at the end of the heating season and used again if stored carefully for the summer.

Single thickness, heavy-duty polythene lets through plenty of light, and is cheap to buy, but it is not the most effective material for conserving heat.

Bubble polythene is more efficient because air trapped in the bubbles cuts down heat loss. If possible, choose bubble polythene that is thick, with large pockets of air. It lets through less light, but is more efficient at reducing heat loss.

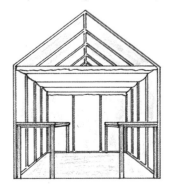

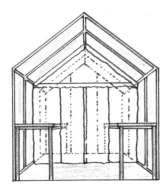

LATE AUTUMN

A LAST-MINUTE SPURT OF ACTION is often needed at this time of year, to get the garden ready for winter and ensure protection for plants that need it. In colder areas, winter will have already arrived, but in warmer climes, there are still many mild days to be enjoyed. Make the most of them while they last!

JOBS IN BRIEF

The Kitchen Garden

❑ Protect late cauliflowers from frost by bending surrounding leaves over the head
❑ Use cloches to protect vulnerable vegetables from cold weather
❑ Winter dig, especially heavy soils
❑ Prune black currants, gooseberries and raspberries
❑ Plant bare-root fruit bushes and trees. Bare-root fruit trees and bushes must be planted while they are dormant. Although container-grown plants may be planted at any time of year, late autumn is the ideal time. You will find an extensive range of plants to choose from in the garden centres at this time of year
❑ Clean and oil tools before putting them away for the winter
❑ Check on stored fruit
❑ Pot up some herbs to give a taste of summer in the winter

The Greenhouse and Conservatory

❑ Clean and disinfect, ready for the winter months

❑ Insulate the greenhouse ready for winter with polythene (plastic) bubble insulation
❑ Check that the minimum temperatures are being achieved with a minimum-maximum thermometer. If you haven't got a thermometer, it is a good idea to buy one
❑ Ventilate the greenhouse whenever the weather is mild enough because stale air can encourage diseases in some cases
❑ Fumigation is an excellent way to control a number of pests that may be lurking in nooks and crannies around the greenhouse

TOP: *Insulating the greenhouse is especially important during the cold winter months, helping to keep heating costs down as well as preventing any violent fluctuations in temperature that could affect the plants inside. Polythene (plastic) bubble insulation is cheap and efficient.*

RIGHT: *When planting fruit trees and bushes, ensure that the plant is firmed in well.*

POT UP HERBS FOR WINTER USE

You don't have to make do with dried or frozen herbs just because it is winter. Some herbs, such as mint, chives, parsley and marjoram, can be potted up to grow indoors or in the greenhouse for a fresh supply of winter leaves. The supply will be modest, but no less welcome.

1 Mint is an easy plant to force indoors, or in a cold frame or greenhouse. Lift an established clump to provide a supply of roots to pot up.

2 Be careful to select only pieces with healthy leaves (diseased leaves are common by the end of the season). You can pull pieces off by hand or cut through them with a knife.

3 Plant the roots in a pot if you want to try to keep the plant growing indoors for a month or so longer. Three-quarters fill a 20–25cm (8–10in) pot with soil or potting soil, then spread the roots out and cover with more soil.

4 If you want a supply of tender fresh leaves early next spring, cut off the tops and put the roots in seed trays or deeper boxes, then cover them with soil. If you keep them in a greenhouse (or even a protected cold frame) you will be able to harvest new mint much earlier.

5 Chives also respond favourably to lifting for an extended season. Lift a small clump to pot up. If it's too large, you should be able to pull it apart into smaller pieces.

6 Place the clump in a pot of ordinary garden soil or potting soil, firm well, and water thoroughly. It should continue to provide leaves after those outdoors have died back, and will produce new ones earlier next spring.

PARSLEY AND MARJORAM

If you cut down and pot up marjoram, it will usually spring into new growth provided warmth and light are right.

Parsley is always a dependable winter herb if grown from a late summer or autumn sowing and kept on a windowsill.

AUTUMN CLEAN THE GREENHOUSE

Autumn is an ideal time to clean the greenhouse. It is likely to be less full than in spring, and it is important to start the season of cold, dull days with clean glass to allow in all available light, and an environment as free as possible of pests and diseases.

1 If you have not already removed the remains of summer shading, do it as soon as possible. Shading washes like this are easy to wipe off with a duster if dry.

2 Whether or not summer shading has been used, clean the glass. The easiest way to clean the outside is with a brush or cleaning head on a long handle. Spray with water, adding a little detergent if necessary, and rub clean. Rinse with clean water.

LEFT: *Even if the greenhouse is still filled with colour, autumn is a good time to give the structure, shelves and benches a thorough clean.*

3 A proprietary glass cleaner will be very effective in removing dirt and grime, but is usually only practical for a small greenhouse where you can easily reach the glass. Clean the glass inside as well as out.

4 Algae often grow where the panes of glass overlap, an area that also traps dirt. Try squirting a jet of water between the panes, then dislodge the dirt with a thin strip of rigid plastic (a plastic plant label usually works well).

5 Finally, squirt another jet of water between the panes to move the loosened dirt and algae.

6 Dirt and soil also accumulate where the glass joins the base, and this can be a breeding ground for pests and diseases. Use a label or a small tool to lift the soil out of the crevice, then douse with a garden disinfectant (keep away from plants).

7 Fumigation is a good way to control a number of pests and diseases that may be lurking in nooks and crannies around the greenhouse. You may be able to keep some or all of the plants in, or you can fumigate an empty greenhouse. Check the label.

8 It is worth disinfecting the frame and staging, whether or not you fumigate the greenhouse. Rather than use a household disinfectant, use one sold for the garden and greenhouse.

9 Diseases are easily carried over from one plant to another on old pots and seed trays. When you have a moment between now and spring, wash them all in a garden disinfectant, scrubbing them well. The inside is as important as the outside.

WINTER

*As the frosty fingers of winter begin to close in on autumn,
the warmth of the armchair naturally becomes increasingly appealing to
most gardeners. But winter should not be a time of inaction in the
kitchen garden. Important tasks such as digging over the vegetable plot,
pruning fruit trees and bushes and testing the soil should all be carried
out as the year draws to a close. Even in the starkest of winters,
resourceful gardeners will be able keep the garden productive. Crops such
as leeks, kale, chicory and swedes can still be enjoyed, and, with the
aid of your greenhouse, new varieties of raspberries and strawberries will
be ready to eat in the darkest winter months.*

ABOVE: *Freshly dug potatoes and beetroot (beets)
in a hand-painted trug after harvesting.*

OPPOSITE: *The exotically colourful purple Brussels
sprout contrasts with* Dahlia *'Bishop of Landaff'.*

EARLY WINTER

THE ONSET OF WINTER INEVITABLY means fewer jobs to do in the garden, but try and get outdoors whenever the weather is favourable. There is always tidying-up to be done, things such as fences to be mended, and now is a good time to think about improving your soil. Crops such as parsnips and swedes can still be enjoyed.

JOBS IN BRIEF

The Kitchen Garden

❑ Test your soil and apply lime if necessary
❑ Dig over the vegetable plot
❑ Prune black currants, gooseberries and raspberries
❑ Plant bare-root fruit bushes and trees while they are dormant
❑ Check the condition of canes and stakes, and clean them up if necessary. Stand the ends in a wood preservative for a day if not already done so
❑ Finish picking late apples
❑ Lift leeks and parsnips as required for use. If the weather is severe, lift leeks in a mild period and heel in so that they are easy to lift when the ground is frozen
❑ Start forcing rhubarb

The Greenhouse and Conservatory

❑ Once a week, check all plants and pick off any dead or dying leaves
❑ Ventilate on warm days, especially if the greenhouse is well insulated, to discourage disease
❑ Check temperatures
❑ Clean the glass to make the most of poor winter light

TOP LEFT: *A terracotta rhubarb forcer.*

TOP RIGHT: *Add lime to soil in winter if tests show it is necessary.*

RIGHT: *Winter digging the vegetable plot.*

CROPS IN SEASON

- **Brussels sprouts** (for details on harvesting, see early autumn).
- **Cabbages** (for details on harvesting, see late autumn).
- **Carrots** (for details on harvesting, see mid summer).
- **Celeriac** (for details on harvesting, see mid autumn).
- **Celery** (for details on harvesting, see late summer).
- **Chard** (for details on harvesting, see late summer).
- **Chicory** The best known variety of chicory is probably Witloof or Belgian chicory, which is grown mainly for the tight-leaved "chicons". These are the forced and blanched new shoots produced from chicory roots. The roots can be lifted now in preparation for storage and forcing (for details on forcing and blanching, see mid winter).
- **Kale** (for details on harvesting, see late autumn).
- **Leeks** (for details on harvesting, see mid autumn).
- **Lettuces** Harvest loose leaf types a few at a time.
- **Parsnips** (for details on harvesting, see mid autumn).
- **Raspberries** Varieties have been developed to supply fruit from early summer right through to the first frosts, which in a mild year can mean early winter. Rather than having three separate rows, divide a single row into three or even four separate sections. (For details on harvesting, see early summer).
- **Salsify** and **scorzonera** (for details on harvesting, see mid autumn).

- **Spinach** (for details on harvesting, see mid autumn and late spring).
- **Strawberries** Many varieties are now available which can picked from early summer right through to the first frosts. (For details on harvesting, see mid summer).

BELOW: *Picking raspberries.*

BELOW: *Conny lettuces, ready for harvesting.*

- **Swedes (yellow turnips)** (for details on harvesting, see early autumn).
- **Turnips** (for details on harvesting, see mid autumn and late spring).
- **Winter radishes** (for details on harvesting, see mid autumn).

BELOW: *Always ensure the greenhouse is kept clean.*

WINTER DIG THE VEGETABLE PLOT

If you have a vegetable plot, or other large area of ground that requires digging, this is a good time to do it. If the soil is a heavy clay, leaving it rough-dug over the winter will allow frost and the weather to help break down large clods. This will make it easier to rake level and to produce a seedbed of fine, crumbly soil in spring. You may prefer to leave digging a light, sandy soil until spring, as this type of soil tends to become flattened and compacted by winter rain if dug too early. New weed growth may also be a problem by spring and can be dealt with at the same time.

1 Divide the space to be dug in half lengthways, marking the area with string. Dividing the plot like this avoids moving excavated soil from one end of the plot to the other.

2 Take out a trench the depth and width of a spade blade. Pile the soil at the end of the other half of the plot, as shown.

3 When you remove the next trench, throw the soil forward into the space left by the first. Digging is easier if you first 'cut' a slice the width of the bite of soil to be dug.

4 Push the spade in parallel to the trench, taking a slice of soil about 15–20cm (6–8in) deep. Larger bites may be too heavy to lift comfortably.

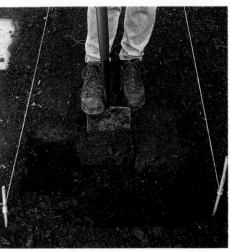

5 Loosen the soil by pulling back on the handle, while trying to keep the bite of soil on the spade.

6 Flick the soil over with the wrist, inverting the clod of earth so that the top is buried. Lift with your knees, not your back.

7 When the end of the plot is reached, fill the trench with soil taken from the first row of the return strip.

8 Finally, fill the trench left when digging has been completed with the soil put on one side from the initial excavation.

DOUBLE DIGGING

Single digging is adequate for most plants, and adding manure or garden compost in this top layer is likely to do more good for short-rooted plants like lettuces and cabbages than burying it deeply. However, for certain deep-rooted crops, such as runner beans, or to break up neglected ground, double digging can be useful. Bear in mind that it also doubles the effort!

1 Divide the plot up in the same way as described for single digging, and deal with the soil from the end of each strip in the same way. But this time make the trenches about 40cm (16in) wide and 25cm (10in) deep.

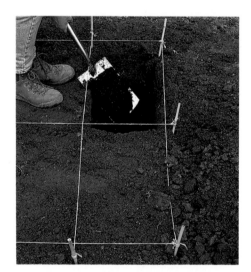

2 Spread a generous layer of well-rotted manure or garden compost – or other bulky organic material that will retain moisture and add humus – over the bottom of the trench.

3 Fork this thick layer of manure or organic material into the bottom of the trench. A fork is better than a spade because it will penetrate the harder lower layer more easily and will mix the material into the soil better.

4 Move the garden line to the next position, maintaining the same 40cm (16in) spacing, or thereabouts. Cut and slice the soil and throw it forward as before, but take several bites per strip, otherwise the soil will be too heavy.

TEST YOUR SOIL

Many people garden successfully without ever testing their soil, but they are probably fortunate in gardening on ground that is not deficient in nutrients, is neither too acid nor too alkaline, and receives plenty of nutrients anyway as part of normal cultivation. If things don't seem to be growing well, a soil test is the best starting point for putting things right, and keen growers test their soil routinely once a year.

Professional soil testing is the most accurate for nutrients, but you can get a reasonable idea of the major nutrients in your soil with simple indicator kits. Testing for pH (see the box opposite) is quick and effective.

Bear in mind that kits vary from one manufacturer to another, so always follow the manufacturer's instructions if they vary from the advice given here.

1 Collect the soil sample from about 5–8cm (2–3in) below the surface. This gives a more typical reading of nutrient levels in the root area. Take a number of samples from around the garden, but test each one separately.

2 With this kit one part of soil is mixed with five parts of water. Shake together vigorously in a clean jar, then allow the water to settle. This can take between half an hour and a day, depending on the soil.

3 Draw off some settled liquid from the top few centimetres (about an inch) for your test.

4 Carefully transfer the solution to the test and reference chambers in the plastic container, using the pipette provided.

5 Select the appropriate colour-coded capsule (different ones are used for each major nutrient) and empty the powder it contains into the test chamber. Replace the cap, then shake vigorously.

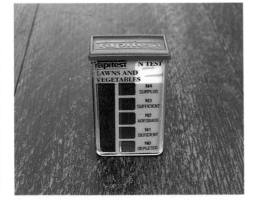

6 After a few minutes, compare the colour of the liquid with the shade panel that forms part of the container. The kit contains an explanation of the significance of each reading, and what – if anything – to do.

WHAT IS pH?

The term pH is a scientific way of stating how acid or alkaline something is. Soils vary in their degree of acidity or alkalinity. The scale runs from 0 (most acid) to 14 (most alkaline), with 7 as neutral. Soils never reach these extremes, and horticulturally, 6.5 can be considered neutral in that it is the pH at which most plants will grow happily. Acid-loving plants, such as rhododendrons, camellias, peonies (see above) and heathers, need a lower pH and may develop chlorosis – a yellowing of the leaves – if grown on chalky soil. Chalk-loving plants like dianthus and lilacs prefer a pH of 7 or above.

These differences may sound small, but on the pH scale 1 point represents a ten-fold increase in acidity or alkalinity.

TESTING THE pH

Collect your samples and mix with water as described for nutrient testing, but for the pH test you don't have to wait for the mixture to settle, and only the test chamber is filled with the solution. Clean tap water is used for the reference chamber. Add the indicator chemical provided with the kit, then put the top on and shake vigorously. Compare the colour with the shade panel on the container for the nearest pH value.

USING PROBE METERS

Probes that measure the pH on a dial are very quick and easy to use, but some people consider them less accurate than colour indicator tests. To ensure an accurate reading, follow the instructions and keep the tip clean.

Push the probe into the soil, and take the reading once the needle seems to have settled. Take several readings from the same area to check results, then move on to another part of the garden.

ADDING LIME TO THE SOIL

Never add lime unless you have tested your soil first and know that it is necessary. Too much lime applied regularly can be harmful for your plants. Always check that you are applying the right sort of lime at the appropriate application rate. Your testing kit should contain advice about how much lime (which will vary with type) to apply to your soil to adjust the pH.

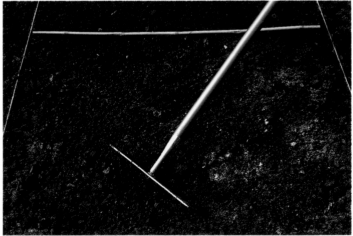

1 Hydrated lime, often used for gardens, should not be handled unnecessarily. Always use gloves, and goggles to protect your eyes. Ground limestone is safer to handle.

2 Rake the lime into the surface, whichever kind of lime you use.

MID WINTER

IF YOU HAVE NOT ALREADY DONE SO, now is the time to undertake jobs such as digging and tidying up the garden ready for the new year. Check the soil if you have not already done so, and add lime if necessary. Many crops like broad beans can be sown with the aid of cloches, and now is the time to think about forcing rhubarb.

JOBS IN BRIEF

The Kitchen Garden

❑ This is the ideal time to test your soil. There is a range of kits available for the job
❑ Apply lime if the test indicates that your soil needs it
❑ Continue winter digging
❑ Force rhubarb and chicory
❑ Sow broad beans under cloches during mild spells

The Greenhouse and Conservatory

❑ Once a week, check all plants and pick off any dead or dying leaves before they start to rot
❑ Ventilate on warm days

ABOVE: *Remember to compost any organic waste. Keep the compost bin covered with an old mat or a sheet of polythene (sheet vinyl or plastic).*

TOP RIGHT: *Make sure the heaters in the greenhouse are working properly to maintain the correct minimum temperature.*

RIGHT: *Sow broad (fava) beans under cloches, but only during mild spells.*

CROPS IN SEASON

- **Brussels sprouts** (for details on harvesting, see early autumn).
- **Cabbages** (for details on harvesting, see late autumn).
- **Carrots** (for details on harvesting, see mid summer).
- **Celeriac** (for details on harvesting, see mid autumn).
- **Celery** (for details on harvesting, see late summer).
- **Chard** (for details on harvesting, see late summer).

- **Chicory** (for details on harvesting, see early winter).
- **Kale** (for details on harvesting, see late autumn).
- **Leeks** (for details on harvesting, see mid autumn).
- **Lettuces** (for details on harvesting, see early winter and late spring).
- **Parsnips** (for details on harvesting, see mid autumn).

- **Salsify and scorzonera** (for details on harvesting, see mid autumn).
- **Swedes (yellow turnips)** (for details on harvesting, see early autumn).
- **Turnips** (for details on harvesting, see mid autumn and late spring).
- **Winter radishes** (for details on harvesting, see mid autumn).

BELOW: *Swiss chard.*

BELOW: *Brussel sprouts.*

BELOW: *Watering Celeriac*

FORCE RHUBARB

Rhubarb is one of those crops that almost looks after itself, and if you have an established clump, forcing tender young stems is very easy. There are many methods of forcing rhubarb, and they all seem to work well. Just choose a technique that you find convenient.

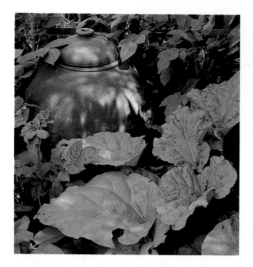

ABOVE: *Rhubarb is a useful early crop that you can start forcing now. A terracotta forcing pot is shown in the background.*

1 Choose a method of excluding light. Special pots were once used for this, but now most people improvise. An old tea chest, bucket or barrel are simple but effective alternatives. If you don't have these, make a frame from wire-netting and canes as shown here.

2 Pile straw into the wire-netting cage, pressing it well down, to provide warmth and protection.

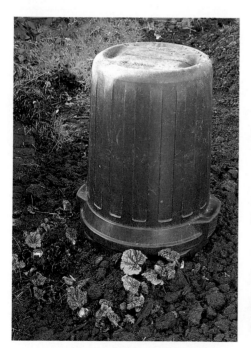

3 Another simple way to make a rhubarb forcer is with a plastic dustbin. If you don't mind cutting the bottom out of it, use it the right way up with a lid on, otherwise use it inverted without a lid.

4 For really early crops many gardeners lift a well-established root to leave on the surface for a few weeks. This gives the root a cold spell that makes it think winter is more advanced than it is.

5 Replant your chilled crown for outdoor forcing, or bring it into the greenhouse. If you have a warm greenhouse, place it under the bench, screened with black plastic. Alternatively, pot it up and put in a plastic bag to take indoors. Make sure there is plenty of air in the bag by keeping it loose and making a few small air holes, then place the bag in a warm yet convenient place – under the stairs or in a kitchen cupboard. Check progress periodically.

FORCE CHICORY

Chicons, the forced and blanched new shoots produced from chicory roots, are an enjoyable winter vegetable when fresh produce is scarce. It is best if you grow your own roots from plants sown in late spring or early summer, but you may be able to buy roots for forcing.

1 To produce chicons, you should choose a variety of chicory recommended for the purpose – 'Witloof' is an old and traditional variety. Lift the root from mid autumn onwards, and leave on the surface for a few days.

2 When the roots have been exposed for a few days, which helps to retard growth, trim the tops off to leave a 3–5cm (1–2in) stump of growth. You can pot them up now or store them in a box of sand, peat or dry soil for use later.

3 To force, place three roots in a 23cm (9in) pot, using a moist potting soil or ordinary garden soil. You may have to trim the ends of the roots to fit them in the pot. Leave the crowns exposed.

Cover the pot with a second pot with the drainage holes blocked (use a piece of kitchen foil for this), and keep in a temperature of 10–18°C (50–65°F). Keep the compost just moist. The chicons will be ready in about three weeks.

WRITING LABELS IN ADVANCE

It makes sense to do as many jobs as you can in winter that will save time later when you are busy sowing and planting. Instead of waiting, write your labels on a day when you can't get into the garden. You will probably make a neater job of it by doing it more leisurely, and it will take pressure off the time when you're busy in the garden.

WINTER PROTECTION

Although most of the plants left in the garden at this time of year are hardy, there may well be some plants still in need of protection. If your garden is a cold one and the soil does not warm up until late in the spring, there are several things that you can do to improve the situation.

FROST

Winter cold is not generally too much of a problem in the vegetable garden because most of the plants that are left are hardy. In very cold areas or in cold spells it is a good idea to protect permanent crops, such as globe artichokes, by covering them with straw.

There is more of a problem if the garden is a cold one and the soil does not warm up until late in the spring. If your garden is like this, you will find it impossible to start gardening until then, and this makes early crops difficult to grow. There are several things you can do to help plants in a cold garden.

1 Some plants, such as globe artichokes, are hardy but can be damaged by severe weather. They can be covered with straw to give them extra protection.

2 Filling a box with straw makes a good form of insulation that can be removed and replaced. It also prevents the straw being blown about.

3 Cloches provide longer term protection. They can be used to protect crops through the winter or as temporary cover whenever frosts threaten more vulnerable plants.

4 If a frost pocket is caused by a thick hedge stopping cold air from rolling down a hill, cut a hole in the base so that the air can pass through and continue down the hill away from the garden.

WIND

Winds can be destructive. Not only can they knock over and break plants, but wind-rock can also cause a plant to move about so that it becomes loose in the soil. Wind can even create a hole around the point at which the plant enters the soil. This fills with stagnant water and the plant can rot. Cold winds can create wind–burn, which shrivels leaves. There are several steps you can take to minimize the damage.

Walls stop the wind dead, but turbulence can be created as the wind escapes over the top, and this can be more destructive than the wind itself. A hedge provides excellent protection from the wind. It allows some air to flow through, thus reducing the turbulence. Turbulence is also reduced considerably by the use of double hedges or two rows of windbreaks. Set a few metres/yards apart, these will give far greater protection than a single barrier.

BELOW: *Hedges are a great form of protection against the wind, negating its most harmful aspects without creating turbulence. As a rule, a hedge will create a wind shadow of about ten times the height of the barrier. The degree of protection decreases the further you get from the hedge.*

LATE WINTER

IN FAVOURABLE AREAS LATE WINTER can be almost spring-like, but don't be lulled into sowing and planting outdoors too soon. If the weather turns very cold, seeds won't germinate and seedlings and plants will receive a severe check to their growth. Concentrate on indoor sowing and use cloches and frames for early crops.

JOBS IN BRIEF

The Kitchen Garden

- ❑ Finish winter digging
- ❑ Apply manures and fertilizers
- ❑ Force rhubarb
- ❑ Sow broad (fava) beans and summer radishes under cloches
- ❑ Plant shallots
- ❑ Warm up the soil using cloches
- ❑ Sow early crops in cold frames or beneath cloches
- ❑ Prepare runner bean and celery trenches for an impressive crop
- ❑ Chit "seed" potatoes (small tubers) of early varieties
- ❑ Plant new fruit trees
- ❑ Mulch established fruit trees and bushes with garden compost or rotted manure
- ❑ Put cloches over strawberries if you want an early crop
- ❑ If peach leaf curl is a problem, spray peaches and nectarines with a recommended fungicide

The Greenhouse and Conservatory

- ❑ Increase ventilation on warm days.
- ❑ Make sure the glass is clean so the plants receive plenty of light

TOP LEFT: *It is best to avoid working on wet soil, but sometimes it is necessary. To ensure that the soil is not compacted and its structure destroyed, it is advisable to work from a plank of wood.*

TOP RIGHT: *Ventilate greenhouses on warm days.*

RIGHT: *Finish any winter digging in preparation for the new season.*

CROPS IN SEASON

❏ **Broccoli.** Depending on variety, harvesting starts in late winter to mid–spring. Snap or cut off the shoots as they begin to bud up but before they come into flower. Shoots should be about 15cm/6in long. Pick the shoots from all parts of the plant. Do not allow any to come into flower, or they will quickly run to seed and exhaust the plant.

❏ **Cabbages** (for details on harvesting, see late autumn).

❏ **Carrots** (for details on harvesting, see mid summer).

❏ **Celeriac** (for details on harvesting, see mid autumn).

❏ **Chard** (for details on harvesting, see late summer).

❏ **Forced chicory** (for details on harvesting, see mid winter).

❏ **Kale** (for details on harvesting, see late autumn).

❏ **Leeks** (for details on harvesting, see mid autumn).

❏ **Lettuces** (for details on harvesting, see early winter and late spring).

❏ **Parsnips** (for details on harvesting, see mid autumn).

❏ **Winter radishes** (for details on harvesting, see mid autumn).

BELOW: *Cabbage.*

BELOW: *Parsnips.*

BELOW: *Harvesting broccoli.*

SOW EARLY CROPS IN YOUR COLD FRAME

If your cold frame is not packed with over-wintering plants, make use of it for early vegetable crops. Radishes and turnips are among the crops that grow quickly and mature early in a cold frame, but you can also try forcing varieties of carrot. Suitable varieties of lettuce also do well.

1 Dig over the ground in the frame, working in as much organic material as possible. Farmyard manure is useful for enriching the soil for these early crops. Do not apply powerful artificial fertilizers at this time.

2 Rake the soil level, and make shallow drills with the rake or a hoe. You can sow the seeds broadcast (scattered randomly), but this makes weeding and thinning more difficult.

3 Sow the seeds thinly, then rake the soil back over the drills. Water thoroughly, then keep the frame closed until the seeds germinate. Once they are through, ventilate on mild days, but keep closed, and if possible insulated, at night.

WARM UP THE SOIL

If you have a kitchen garden, start warming up the soil with cloches to get your vegetables off to an early start. Although most early vegetables are not sown until early spring, you need to have your cloches in position several weeks before you plan to sow.

1 Cloche designs vary considerably, but most can easily be made into long runs the length of the row. Make sure that they are butted close together and that plastic cloches are well anchored to the ground.

2 End pieces are essential, otherwise the cloches will just become a wind tunnel. Make sure they are fixed firmly in place.

3 Polythene tunnel cloches are inexpensive to buy, and although they need to be re-covered after a few seasons, a replacement sheet is inexpensive. Fix the hoops first, then stretch the sheet over them.

4 Use the special fixing wires to hold the sheet in position.

5 Secure the ends with sticks or pegs, pulling the plastic taut.

6 Heap a little soil over the edges to anchor the cloches.

PREPARE BEAN AND CELERY TRENCHES

You can grow a satisfactory crop of beans without special soil preparation, and achieve a respectable crop of self-blanching celery by planting on ground that has not been specially enriched. But if you want an especially heavy and impressive crop, it is worth preparing the trench.

1 Take out a trench 25–30cm (10–12in) deep and 60cm (2ft) wide for runner beans, 38cm (15in) wide for celery. Heap the soil to one or both sides of the trench.

2 Add as much rotted manure or garden compost as you can spare. This will add some nutrients and benefit the structure and moisture-holding capacity of the soil.

3 Fork the manure or garden compost into the soil at the bottom of the trench – don't leave it as a layer. Finally, rake the soil back into the trench.

APPLY SLOW-ACTING FERTILIZERS

Apply slow-acting fertilizers such as bonemeal and proprietary controlled-release fertilizers when the vegetable plot has been dug and levelled, ready for sowing from early spring onwards. Controlled-release fertilizers release their nutrients only when the soil is warm enough for the plants to use them. Fertilizers should always be applied evenly and at the recommended rate.

1 Divide the area into strips 1m or 1yd wide with string, and space canes at the same interval to form a square. Scatter the measured dose, then move the canes. Rake into the soil.

SUPPLIERS

The following names and addresses are useful first contacts for many of the plants and gardening accessories, such as greenhouses and watering systems, that you may need to buy. In the space available, however, we can give only a small selection, and in most cases there are many more excellent suppliers that could be mentioned. Don't forget that the best place to start when looking for tools and equipment and an initial selection of plants is often your local garden centre. Frequently they can obtain items that are not in stock, or they may be able to suggest a suitable supplier.

UNITED KINGDOM

GARDEN EQUIPMENT AND SUPPLIES

Atco-Qualcast Ltd
Suffolk Works
Stowmarket
Suffolk
IP14 1EY
Tel: 01449 612183
Lawnmowers, powered rakes and hedge trimmers

Black and Decker
Westpoint
The Grove
Slough
SL1 1QQ
Tel: 01753 511234
Powered tools

Gardena UK Ltd
Unit 7
Dunhams Court
Dunhams Lane
Letchworth
Hertfordshire
SG6 1BD
Tel: 01462 686688
Watering systems, hand and powered tools

Sandvik Ltd
Manor Way
Halesowen
West Midlands
B62 8QZ
Tel: 0121 550 4700
Pruning tools and equipment

Two Wests & Elliott Ltd
Unit 4, Carrwood Road
Sheepbridge Industrial Estate
Chesterfield
Derbyshire S41 9RH
Tel: 01246 451077
Greenhouse accessories, watering systems

Wolf Tools for Garden & Lawn Ltd
Alton Road
Ross-on-Wye
Herefordshire HR9 5NE
Tel: 01989 767600
Garden and lawn tools

SEEDS AND NURSERIES

Iden Croft Herbs
Frittenden Road
Staplehurst
Kent TN12 0DH
Tel: 01580 891432

S.E. Marshall & Co Ltd
Regal Road
Wisbech
Cambridgeshire
PR13 2RF
Tel: 01945 583407

Sutton Seeds Ltd
Hele Road
Torquay
Devon TQ2 7QJ
Tel: 01803 614455

Thomson & Morgan UK (Ltd)
Poplar Lane
Ipswich
Suffolk
IP8 3BU
Tel: 01473 688821

GREENHOUSES AND CONSERVATORIES

Amdega Ltd
Faverdale
Darlington
Co. Durham DL3 0PW
Tel: 01325 468522

Banbury Homes and Gardens
PO Box 17
Banbury
Oxfordshire OX17 3NS

S. Wernick & Sons Ltd
Lindon Road
Brownhills
Walsall
West Midlands
WS8 7BW

AUSTRALIA

GARDEN EQUIPMENT AND SUPPLIES

Centre Landscaping and Supplies
Ross Highway
Alice Springs NT 5750
Tel : (089) 52 4839

The Happy Gardener
13 Aldous Place
Melville WA 6156
Tel : (09) 317 2520

Sherwyn
53-55 Canterbury Road
Montrose VIC 3765
Tel : (03) 728 9676

SEEDS AND NURSERIES

Australian Seed Company
5 Rosedale Avenue
Hazelbrook
NSW 2779

Arnhem Nursery
35 Arnhem Highway
Humpty Doo
NT 5791
Tel: (089) 88 1351

Perrots Nursery
Deception Bay Road
QLD 4508
Tel : (07) 888 3737

Warren Glen Nursuries
373 Ringwood–
  Warrandyte Road
Warrandyte
VIC 3113
Tel: (03) 844 3027

Yarralumla Nursery
Banks Street
Yarralumla
ACT
2600
Tel : (06) 207 2444

NEW ZEALAND

GARDEN EQUIPMENT AND SUPPLIES

California Green World Garden Centre
139 Park Road
Miramar
Wellington
Tel: (04) 388 3260

Palmers Garden World
Cr. Shore & Orakei Roads
Remuera
Auckland
Tel: (09) 524 4038

NURSERIES

Big Trees
Coatesville
Auckland
Tel: (09) 415 9983

Kent's Nurseries
Cr. Fergusson Drive & Ranfurly Street
Trentham
Tel: (04) 528 3889

INDEX

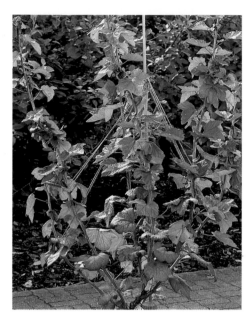

ACKNOWLEDGEMENTS

Specially commissioned photography © Anness Publishing Ltd. All
photography by Peter Anderson except as listed below:

Key: t = top; b = bottom; c = centre; l = left; r = right.

ADDITIONAL PICTURE CREDITS

The publishers would like to thank the following for permission to
reproduce images in the book.

Peter McHoy; 11 tr, b; 24 br; 26 br; 37 br; 49 tr; 59 br; 70 bl;
78 br; 81 br.